JUNIOR HIGH • MIDDLE SCHOOL

TALKSHEETS

Psalms and Proverbs—Updated!

50
DISCUSSION STARTERS
FOR JUNIOR HIGH YOUTH GROUPS

RICK BUNDSCHUH & TOM FINLEY

Youth Specialties

ZONDERVAN™

GRAND RAPIDS, MICHIGAN 49530

D1377187

Junior High–Middle School TalkSheets Psalms and Proverbs—Updated! 50 discussion starters for junior high youth groups.

Copyright © 2001 by Youth Specialties

Youth Specialties books, 300 S. Pierce St., El Cajon, CA 92020, are published by Zondervan, 5300 Patterson Ave. S.E., Grand Rapids, MI 49530

Library of Congress Cataloging-in-Publication Data

Bundschuh, Rick, 1951-
    Junior high, middle school talksheets from Psalms & Proverbs, updated! : 50 creative discussion starters from the Bible / Rick Bundschuh & Tom Finley.
        p. cm.
    ISBN 0-310-23851-X
    1. Bible. O.T. Psalms—Study and teaching. 2. Bible. O.T. Proverbs—Study and teaching. 3. Junior high school students—Religious life. 4. Middle school students—Religious life. 5. Church group work with teenagers. I. Title: Junior high, middle school talk sheets from Psalms & Proverbs, updated. II. Finley, Tom, 1951- III. Title.

BS1451 .B855 2001
223'.2'00712—dc21

                                                                                        00-043933

Web site addresses listed in this book were current at the time of publication, but we can't guarantee they're still operational. If you have trouble with a URL, please contact us via email (YS@YouthSpecialties.com) to let us know if you've found the correct or new URL or if the URL is no longer operational.

Edited by Mary Fletcher, Anita Palmer, and Tamara Rice
Cover and interior design by PAZ Design Group
Illustrations and borders by Rick Sealock

Printed in the United States of America

    02   03   04   05   06   07 / VG / 5   4   3

CONTENTS

JUNIOR HIGH·MIDDLE SCHOOL

Psalms and Proverbs—Updated!

THE HOWS AND WHATS OF TALKSHEETS

You are holding a very valuable book! No, it won't make you a genius or millionaire. But it does contain 50 instant discussions for junior high and middle school kids. Inside you'll find reproducible TalkSheets that cover a variety of hot topics—plus simple, step-by-step instructions on how to use them. All you need is this book, a few copies of the hand-outs, and some kids (and maybe a snack or two). You're on your way to landing on some serious issues in kids' lives today.

These TalkSheets are user-friendly and very flexible. They can be used in a youth group meeting, a Sunday school class, or in a Bible study group. You can adapt them for either large or small groups. And, they can be covered in only 20 minutes or explored more intensively in two hours.

You can build an entire youth group meeting around a single TalkSheet, or you can use TalkSheets to supplement other materials and resources you might be using. These are tools for you—how you use them is your choice.

Junior High-Middle School TalkSheets Psalms and Proverbs—Updated! is not your average curriculum or workbook. This collection of discussions will get your kids involved and excited about talking through important issues. The TalkSheets deal with key topics and include interesting activities, challenging questions, and eye-catching graphics. They will challenge your kids to think about opinions, learn about themselves, and grow in their faith.

LEADING A TALKSHEET DISCUSSION

TalkSheets can be used as a curriculum for your youth group, but they are designed to be springboards for discussion. They encourage your kids to take part and interact with each other while talking about real life issues. And hopefully they'll do some serious thinking,

discover new ideas for themselves, defend their points of view, and make decisions.

Youth today face a world of moral confusion. Youth leaders must teach the church's beliefs and values—and also help young people make the right choices in a world with so many options. Teenagers are bombarded with the voices of society and media messages—most of which drown out what they hear from the church.

A TalkSheet discussion works for this very reason. While dealing with the questions and activities on the TalkSheet, your kids will think carefully about issues, compare their beliefs and values with others, and make their own choices. TalkSheets will challenge your group to explain and rework their ideas in a Christian atmosphere of acceptance, support, and growth.

The most common fear of junior high and middle school youth group leaders is, "What will I do if the kids in my group just sit there and don't say anything?" Well, when kids don't have anything to say, it's because they haven't had a chance or time to get their thoughts organized! Most young people haven't developed the ability to think on their feet. Since many are afraid they might sound stupid, they don't know how to voice their ideas and opinions.

The solution? TalkSheets let your kids deal with the issues in a challenging, non-threatening way before the actual discussion begins. They'll have time to organize their thoughts, write them down, and ease their fears about participating. They may even look forward to sharing their answers! Most importantly, they'll (most likely) want to find out what others said and open up to talk through the topics.

If you're still a little leery about the success of a real discussion among your kids, that's okay! The only way to get them rolling is to get them started.

YOUR ROLE AS THE LEADER

The best discussions don't happen by accident. They require careful preparation and a sensitive leader. Don't worry if you aren't experienced or don't have hours to prepare.

TalkSheets are designed to help even the novice leader! The more TalkSheet discussions you lead, the easier it becomes. Keep the following tips in mind when using the TalkSheets as you get your kids talking.

BE CHOOSY

Each TalkSheet deals with a different topic. Choose a TalkSheet based on the needs and the maturity level of your group. Don't feel obligated to use the TalkSheets in the order they appear in this book. Use your best judgment and mix them up however you want—they are tools for you!

TRY IT YOURSELF

Once you have chosen a TalkSheet for your group, answer the questions and do the activities yourself. Imagine your kids' reactions to the TalkSheet. This will help you prepare for the discussion and understand what you are asking them to do. Plus, you'll have some time to think of other appropriate questions, activities, and Bible verses.

GET SOME INSIGHT

On each leader's guide page, you'll find numerous tips and ideas for getting the most out of your discussion. You may want to add some of your own thoughts or ideas in the margins. And, there's room to keep track of the date and the name of your group at the top of the leader's page. You'll also find suggestions for additional activities and discussion questions.

There are some references to Internet links throughout the TalkSheets. These are guides for you to find the resources and information that you need. For additional help, be sure to visit the Youth Specialties Web site at www.YouthSpecialties.com for information on materials and further links to finding what you need.

MAKE COPIES

Kids will need their own copy of the TalkSheet. Only make copies of the student's side of the TalkSheet! The material on the reverse side (the leader's guide) is just for you. You're able to make copies for your group because we've given you permission to do so. U.S. copyright laws have not changed, and it is still mandatory to request permission from a publisher before making copies of other published material. It is against the law not to do so. However, permission is given for you to make copies of this material for your group only, not for every youth group in your state. Thank you for cooperating.

INTRODUCE THE TOPIC

It's important to introduce the topic before you pass out the TalkSheets to your group. Depending on your group, keep it short and to the point. Be careful not to over-introduce the topic, sound preachy, or resolve the issue before you've started. Your goal is to spark their interest and leave plenty of room for discussion.

The best way to do this is verbally. You can tell a story, share an experience, or describe a situation or problem having to do with the topic. You might want to jump-start your group by asking something like, "What is the first thing you think of when you hear the word _____ [insert the topic]?" Then, after a few answers have been given, you can add something like, "Well, it seems we all have different ideas about this subject. Tonight we're going to investigate it a bit further..." Then pass out the TalkSheet and be sure that everyone has a pencil or pen. Now you're on your way! The following are excellent methods you can use to introduce any topic in this book—

- Show a related short film or video.
- Read a passage from a book or magazine that relates to the subject.
- Play a popular CD that deals with the topic.
- Perform a short skit or dramatic presentation.
- Play a simulation game or role-play, setting up the topic.
- Present current statistics, survey results, or read a current newspaper article that provides recent information about the topic.
- Use an icebreaker or other crowd game, getting into the topic in a humorous way. For example if the topic is fun, play a game to begin the discussion. If the topic is success, consider a

game that helps the kids experience success or failure.

- Use posters, videos, or any other visuals to help focus attention on the topic.

There are endless possibilities for an intro—you are limited only by your own creativity! Each TalkSheet offers a few suggestions, but you are free to use any method with which you feel most comfortable. But do keep in mind that the introduction is a very important part of each session.

SET BOUNDARIES

It'll be helpful to set a few ground rules before the discussion. Keep the rules to a minimum, of course, but let the kids know what's expected of them. Here are suggestions for some basic ground rules—

- **What is said in this room stays in this room.** Emphasize the importance of confidentiality. Some kids will open up, some won't. Confidentiality is vital for a good discussion. If your kids can't keep the discussion in the room, then they won't open up.
- **No put-downs.** Mutual respect is important. If your kids disagree with some opinions, ask them to comment on the subject (but not on the other person). It's okay to attack the ideas, but not other people.
- **There is no such thing as a dumb question.** Your group members must feel free to ask questions at any time. The best way to learn is to ask questions and get answers.
- **No one is forced to talk.** Let everyone know they have the right to pass or not answer any question.
- **Only one person speaks at a time.** This is a mutual respect issue. Everyone's opinion is worthwhile and deserves to be heard.

Communicate with your group that everyone needs to respect these boundaries. If you sense that your group members are attacking each other or getting a negative attitude during the discussion, do stop and deal with the problem before going on.

ALLOW ENOUGH TIME

Pass out copies of the TalkSheet to your kids after the introduction and make sure that each person has a pen or pencil and a Bible. There are usually five or six activities on each TalkSheet. If your time

is limited, or if you are using only a part of the TalkSheet, tell the group to complete only the activities you'd like them to.

Decide ahead of time whether or not you would like the kids to work on the TalkSheets individually or in groups.

Let them know how much time they have for completing the TalkSheet and let them know when there is a minute (or so) left. Go ahead and give them some extra time and then start the discussion when everyone seems ready to go.

SET THE STAGE

Create a climate of acceptance. Most teenagers are afraid to voice their opinions because they don't want to be laughed at or look stupid in front of their peers. They want to feel safe if they're going to share their feelings and beliefs. Communicate that they can share their thoughts and ideas—even if they may be different or unpopular. If your kids get put-downs, criticism, laughter, or snide comments (even if their statements are opposed to the teachings of the Bible) it'll hurt the discussion.

Always phrase your questions—even those that are printed on the TalkSheets—so that you are asking for an opinion, not an answer. For example if a question reads, "What should Bill have done in that situation?" change it to, "What do you think Bill should have done in that situation?" The simple addition of the three words "do you think" makes the question less threatening and a matter of opinion, rather than a demand for the right answer. Your kids will relax when they will feel more comfortable and confident. Plus, they'll know that you actually care about their opinions and they'll feel appreciated!

LEAD THE DISCUSSION

Discuss the TalkSheet with the group and encourage all your kids to participate. Communicate that it's important for them to respect each other's opinions and feelings! The more they contribute, the better the discussion will be.

If your youth group is big, you may divide it into smaller groups of six to 12. Each of these small groups should have a facilitator—either an adult leader or a student member—to keep the discussion going. Remind the facilitators not to dominate the others. If the group looks to the facilitator for an answer, ask him or her to direct the questions or responses back to the group. Once the smaller groups have completed their discussions, combine them into one large group and ask the different groups to share their ideas.

You don't have to divide the groups up with every TalkSheet. For some discussions, you may want to vary the group size and or divide the meeting into groups of the same sex.

The discussion should target the questions and answers on the TalkSheet. Go through them one at a time and ask the kids to share their responses. Have them compare their answers and brainstorm new ones in addition to the ones they've written down. Encourage them to share their opinions and answers, but don't force those who are quiet.

AFFIRM ALL RESPONSES—RIGHT OR WRONG

Let your kids know that their comments and contributions are appreciated and important. This is especially true for those who rarely speak up in group activities. Make a point of thanking them for joining in. This will be an incentive for them to participate further.

Remember that affirmation doesn't mean approval. Affirm even those comments that seem wrong to you. You'll show that everyone has a right to express their ideas—no matter how controversial they may be. If someone states an opinion that is off base, make a mental note of the comment. Then in your wrap-up, come back to the comment or present a different point of view in a positive way. But don't reprimand the student who voiced the comment.

DON'T BE THE AUTHORITATIVE ANSWER

Some kids think you have the right answer to every question. They'll look to you for approval, even when they are answering another group member's question. If they start to focus on you for answers, redirect them toward the group by making a comment like, "Remember that you're talking to everyone, not just me."

Your goal as the facilitator is to keep the discussion alive and kicking. It's important that your kids think of you as a member of the group—on their level. The less authoritative you are, the more value your own opinions will have. If your kids view you as a peer, they will listen to your comments. You have a tremendous responsibility to be, with sincerity, their trusted friend.

LISTEN TO EACH PERSON

God gave you one mouth and two ears. Good discussion leaders know how to listen. Although it's tempting at times, don't monopolize the discussion. Encourage others to talk first— then express your opinions during your wrap up.

DON'T FORCE IT

Encourage all your kids to talk, but don't make them comment. Each member has the right to pass. If you feel that the discussion isn't going well, go on to the next question or restate the question to keep them moving.

DON'T TAKE SIDES

You'll probably have different opinions expressed in the group from time to time. Be extra careful not to take one side or another. Encourage both sides to think through their positions—ask questions to get them deeper. If everyone agrees on an issue, you can play devil's advocate with tough questions and stretch their thinking. Remain neutral—your point of view is your own, not that of the group.

DON'T LET ANYONE (INCLUDING YOU) TAKE OVER

Nearly every youth group has one person who likes to talk and is perfectly willing to express an opinion on any subject. Try to encourage equal participation from all the kids.

SET UP FOR THE TALK

Make sure that the seating arrangement is inclusive and encourages a comfortable, safe atmosphere for discussion. Theater-style seating (in rows) isn't discussion-friendly. Instead, arrange the chairs in a circle or semicircle (or on the floor with pillows!).

LET THEM LAUGH!

Discussions can be fun! Most of the TalkSheets include questions that'll make them laugh and get them thinking, too.

LET THEM BE SILENT

Silence can be a scary for discussion leaders! Some react by trying to fill the silence with a question or a comment. The following suggestions may help you to handle silence more effectively—

- Be comfortable with silence. Wait it out for 30 seconds or so to respond. You may want to restate the question to give your kids a gentle nudge.
- Talk about the silence with the group. What does the silence mean? Do they really not have any comments? Maybe they're confused, embarrassed, or don't want to share.
- Answer the silence with questions or comments like, "I know this is challenging to think about..." or "It's scary to be the first to talk." If you acknowledge the silence, it may break the ice.
- Ask a different question that may be easier to handle or that will clarify the one already posed. But don't do this too quickly without giving them time to think the first one through.

KEEP IT UNDER CONTROL

Monitor the discussion. Be aware if the discussion is going in a certain direction or off track. This can happen fast, especially if the kids disagree or things get heated. Mediate wisely and set the tone that you want. If your group gets bored with an issue, get them back on track. Let the discussion unfold, but be sensitive to your group and who is or is not getting involved.

If a student brings up a side issue that's interesting, decide whether or not to purse it. If discussion is going well and the issue is worth discussion, let them talk it through. But, if things get way off track, say something like, "Let's come back to that subject later if we have time. Right now, let's finish our discussion on..."

BE CREATIVE AND FLEXIBLE

You don't have to follow the order of the questions on the TalkSheet. Follow your own creative instinct. If you find other ways to use the TalkSheets, use them! Go ahead and add other questions or Bible references.

Don't feel pressured to spend time on every single activity. If you're short on time, you can skip some items. Stick with the questions that are the most interesting to the group.

SET YOUR GOALS

TalkSheets are designed to move along toward a goal, but you need to identify your goal in advance. What would you like your young people to learn? What truth should they discover? What is the goal of the session? If you don't know where you're going, it's doubtful you will get there.

BE THERE FOR YOUR KIDS

Some kids may want to talk more with you (you got 'em thinking!). Let them know that you can talk one-on-one with them afterwards.

Communicate to the kids that they can feel free to talk with you about anything with confidentiality. Let them know you're there for them with support and concern, even after the TalkSheet discussion has been completed.

USE THE BIBLE

Most adults believe the Bible has authority over their lives. It's common for adults to start their discussions or to support their arguments with Bible verses. But today's teenagers form their opinions and beliefs from their own life situations first—then they decide how the Bible fits their needs. TalkSheets start with the realities of the adolescent world and then move toward the Bible. You'll be able to show them that the Bible can be their guide and that God does have something to say to them about their own unique situations.

The last activity on each TalkSheet uses Bible verses that were chosen for their application to each issue. But they aren't exhaustive. Feel free to add whatever other verses you think would fit well and add to the discussion.

After your kids read the verses, ask them to think how the verses apply to their lives and summarize the meanings for them.

For example, after reading the passages for "Window to the Soul," you could summarize by saying something like, "God's standards of beauty for a person's inner self are much different than the world's. How can these verses apply to your inner self?"

CLOSE THE DISCUSSION

Present a challenge to the group by asking yourself, "What do I want the kids to remember most from this discussion?" There's your wrap-up! It's important to conclude by affirming the group and offering a summary that ties the discussion together.

Sometimes you won't need a wrap-up. You may want to leave the issue hanging and discuss it in another meeting. That way, your group can think about it more and you can nail down the final ideas later.

TAKE IT FURTHER

On the leader's guide page, you'll find additional discussion activities—labeled More—for following up on the discussion. These aren't a must, but highly recommended. They let the kids reflect upon, evaluate, review, and assimilate what they've learned. These activities may lead to more discussion and better learning.

After you've done the activity, be sure to debrief your kids on the activity, either now or at the next group meeting. A few good questions to ask about the activity are—

- What happened when you did this activity or discussion?

- Was it helpful or a waste of time?

- How did you feel when doing the activity or discussion?

- Did the activity/discussion make you think differently or affect you in any way?

- In one sentence state what you learned from this activity or discussion.

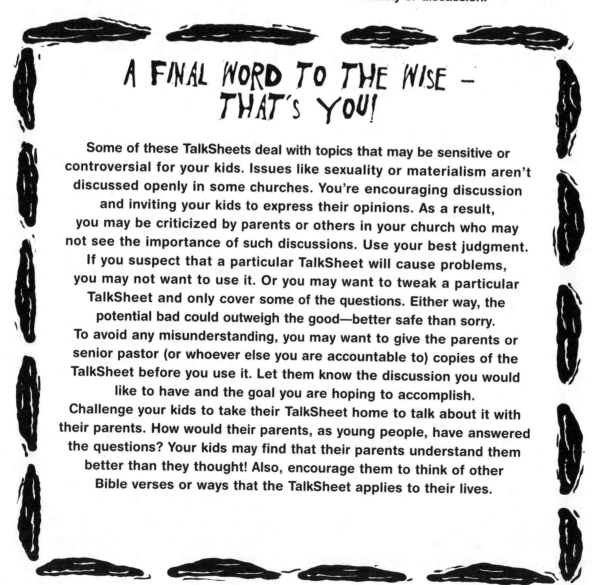

A FINAL WORD TO THE WISE — THAT'S YOU!

Some of these TalkSheets deal with topics that may be sensitive or controversial for your kids. Issues like sexuality or materialism aren't discussed openly in some churches. You're encouraging discussion and inviting your kids to express their opinions. As a result, you may be criticized by parents or others in your church who may not see the importance of such discussions. Use your best judgment.

If you suspect that a particular TalkSheet will cause problems, you may not want to use it. Or you may want to tweak a particular TalkSheet and only cover some of the questions. Either way, the potential bad could outweigh the good—better safe than sorry.

To avoid any misunderstanding, you may want to give the parents or senior pastor (or whoever else you are accountable to) copies of the TalkSheet before you use it. Let them know the discussion you would like to have and the goal you are hoping to accomplish.

Challenge your kids to take their TalkSheet home to talk about it with their parents. How would their parents, as young people, have answered the questions? Your kids may find that their parents understand them better than they thought! Also, encourage them to think of other Bible verses or ways that the TalkSheet applies to their lives.

GOD'S GUIDE TO GODLINESS

1. Have you ever been **lost**?

   What were you looking for when you were lost?

   How did you lose your way?

   What was the first thing you tried, to find your way again?

2. Check out **Psalm 1** and list four things someone like you should do (or not do) to be blessed.
   Verse 1—
   > Do not walk—
   > Do not stand—
   > Do not sit—
   Verse 2—
   > Delight in and think about the—

3. Your friend wants to go over to her boyfriend's house without her parents knowing. So she calls you and tells you that she's coming over to do homework. Her parents think she'll be at your house—only she'll really be at her boyfriend's house.

   What principle(s) from Psalm 1 would you break if you asked her to tell you more about the plan?

   What principle(s) would you break if you helped your friend with her scheme?

   What potentially negative things could happen if you helped her out?

   What might happen if you chose to not go along with your friend's plan?

   If you decided to follow God's guidelines, what would you say to your friend?

4. Think of a negative situation that you or your friends could encounter (it should involve a moral dilemma of some kind such as shoplifting, gossiping, lying, fighting, doing drugs, and so on). On a scale below, indicate with an X how easy it would be for you to *not* get involved in the situation.

   ◆ ▮▮▮▮▮▮▮▮▮▮▮▮▮▮▮▮▮▮▮▮ ◆

   So easy, it wouldn't be an issue   Extremely difficult

GOD'S GUIDE TO GODLINESS [Pursuing godliness—Psalm 1]

THIS WEEK

When it comes down to it, youth workers help kids to choose to live like God would want them to. This TalkSheet gives your students a clear picture of the two roads they can follow in life—one God's way and one their way—and the consequences that can result with each one.

OPENER

Show a photograph of (or describe) someone your students would recognize as an outstanding success in some field, such as athletics. Then do the same for a vile criminal. You'll be able to find plenty of these in a newspaper of on-line news source. How do your kids think these people came to a point of such fame (or infamy)? Point out that it's possible for each person in the room to become the world's greatest athlete or the foulest criminal. The choices they make in life will lead them down certain paths. What paths have these people in the pictures chosen? How did they choose the path they chose? Launch into the TalkSheet discussion by pointing out that the Bible gives some good advice on how to choose the right path in life.

THE DISCUSSION, BY NUMBERS

1. Break your group into pairs or trios for this one. When the groups have finished their discussions, have students share their answers to the TalkSheet's question with the entire class. You may want to jot the principles involved on a whiteboard: "I ran off in the wrong direction," "People missed a landmark," or "People stopped to ask directions." Point out how each relates to going the wrong way or finding the right way.

2. Discuss the principles Psalm 1 gives for making wise and godly decisions. Verse 1 speaks against lending an open ear to tempting words, following others into sin, and mocking (ridiculing or ignoring) God. The second verse talks about the wisdom of basing decisions on God's wisdom, found in the Bible. There are promises—both positive and negative—made in verses 3-6. List the biblical principles for wise decision-making on the whiteboard in preparation for the next item.

3. How did your group respond to this situation? You may want to write some of the pros and cons down on a whiteboard or poster board. Point out that any seemingly harmful things can have devastating results. For example, how would this situation seem if you knew your friend was going to have sex with her boyfriend? What if you knew they'd be drinking or doing drugs? What if you (or your parents) would be held responsible for your friend if anything happened to her?

4. It's sometimes easy for teenagers to see a bad situation—but much harder to stay away from those situations. If you don't want to ask for specific rankings, ask where the group where they think teenagers in general would rank. How about teenagers in the church? Do they think it's easier to resist a bad situation, or get involved? Why or why not?

THE CLOSE

How are your kids struggling in their walk with God? You may want to talk about what is hard about staying on the same path as God. To get them thinking, ask which "road sign" they need to keep their eyes out for. For example, do they need to yield more to God? Stop to think of the consequences? Examine their lives to think if they're going the wrong way? Point out that road signs protect drivers. What road signs does God put up in people's lives to keep them out of danger?

MORE

- Have your students make a map of their spiritual journey—of life's journey. What has their road looked like? Has it been bumpy? Have there been detours along the way? What about mountains of achievement or success in their lives? You may want to have them label the highs and lows along the way and if they feel comfortable, to share a few examples. Point out that everyone's road is bumpy—there are very few easy roads!
- How does Psalm 1 apply to the media today and the society that your kids live in? You may want to spend some time talking with your kids about Christians in the world today. Are Christians involved in the music, TV, or movie industry blessed by God? If so, how? How does the media portray Christians? Is Christianity portrayed as good or bad? Take some time to talk about the struggles of sticking to God's ways when there are so many other distraction. Finally, what do your kids think God would say about this psalm and society today?

FINDING HIS PEACE

1. Life can be nerve-wracking sometimes. Rate the following items from **most nerve-wracking (1)** to **least nerve-wracking (15)**.

___ Being asked to dance when you know you're a klutz
___ Knowing what to do about an abusive situation
___ Forgetting something that was absolutely important
___ Ignoring your parents' rules and getting caught
___ Not having the right clothes to wear
___ Having a family member or friend die
___ Starting first string on the team
___ Being pressured to drink beer at a party
___ Hearing your parents fight and threaten splitting up
___ Knowing how far to go physically with your
___ boyfriend or girlfriend
___ Failing a midterm exam
___ Going to school where kids carry concealed weapons
___ Getting dumped by a friend
___ Asking out the girl or guy that you like
___ Dealing with gang activity at home or school

2. Pick one of the verses below to read. Then describe in your own words what happened in the passage.

2 Samuel 15:1-6
2 Samuel 15:13-14, 23-25, 30-31
2 Samuel 18:24-33

2 Samuel 16:5-14
2 Samuel 18:5-17

3. Now read **Psalm 3**. This was the psalm that King David wrote after the incident with Absalom. David said that even in the midst of the fear and the attacks, he was able to sleep at night. According to David, how was he able to do this?

4. If you were King David, what would you tell this person who was seeking your advice?

Dear King David,
By the last year of grade school, I knew everyone and had lots of friends. Now I'm in a gigantic middle school with tons of kids I don't know. Some of my friends have found new friends. What do I do?

5. Below are some of God's promises from the Bible. Pick **one** of them to rewrite in your own words.

Matthew 6:25-26
John 14:27

John 16:33
Philippians 4:6-7

Colossians 3:15

FINDING HIS PEACE [God's peace—Psalm 3]

THIS WEEK

During the junior high or middle school years, young people experience rapid changes, stress, and confusion. God can get them through it all, serving as a protector and deliverer just as he did to King David so long ago. Students will learn through this TalkSheet how they can place their confidence in God and find peace in him.

OPENER

Start off by asking everyone to stand in the center of the room. Explain that you're going to read some statements. If they agree with a statement, walk to one wall. If they disagree, walking to the another. No one can stay in the center of the room. After each statement, count the number of kids who agreed or disagreed after each of the following statements, and record the results on a whiteboard or poster board.

⇨ The Bible promises that Christians will never have troubles.

⇨ The Bible makes it clear that Christians can't find peace until they go to heaven.

⇨ Any Christian struggling with problems isn't a very good Christian.

⇨ Some Christians never have worries because they can just sit back and watch God solve everything.

⇨ Even the greatest believers must learn to trust God in times of trouble.

Tell your class or group that these questions will be tackled in today's session.

THE DISCUSSION, BY NUMBERS

1. How did your kids rank these situations? You may want to make a list of their rankings. Which problems seem to cause the most anxiety? Which are common to most or all students? Your kids should understand that peace doesn't mean a lack of problems—it means assurance that God will stand with people and help people work through them.

2. David was one of Israel's kings whose son, Absalom, tried to overthrow him by a military attack in which many men were killed. You may want to give each piece of the story to a different group of students. With the group, talk about the fears that David probably felt. What indications do your kids see that David was still seeking God in all of his troubles?

3. What does David say about God in Psalm 3? Point out that God is a shield, he takes care of people, he answers prayer, he sustains, he delivers, he fights on their behalf, and he blesses his people. Then pick the top three or four problems from question 1 and ask your kids how these characteristics of God relate in practical ways to their everyday problems.

4. How would your kids respond to someone, from King David's perspective on God? Some of your kids may be facing the same situation—or worse.

5. Ask for a few volunteers to share how they summarized the verse. You may want to write a few summaries for the group to see. Point out that each of these verses provides encouragement for them in their everyday lives. Encourage them to be encouraged!

THE CLOSE

You might want to give everyone a few minutes to think of one or more areas in which your kids are troubled or are struggling. Point out that God is their shield and deliverer, even when they don't know it. Some of your kids may need someone to talk with—either you or another adult. Be sure to offer yourself to listen to their problems privately. And you may want to give them some time to pray silently for God to give them his peace in their hearts.

MORE

● What enemies do your kids face? Are these enemies people? Pressures to do drugs or be sexually active? Temptations of pornography? You may want to spend time walking with these so-called enemies with your kids. How can your kids deal with these enemies? How Psalm 3 apply to their lives directly?

● Some of your kids may be facing situations that are way beyond nerve-wracking—some that may require professional counseling. Pay attention to your group members. Statistically, some of them may be dealing with physical, sexual, or drug abuse, depression, suicide, and more. If you sense that any students are facing such situations, encourage them to find a trusted adult to talk to. Or if you feel it's necessary, talk with your pastor about contacting the authorities. For more information, National Council on Alcoholism and Drug Dependence, Inc. (http://ncadd.org), Addiction Research Foundation (www.arf.org/isd/info.html), National Exchange Club Foundation (www.preventchildabuse.com), American Humane Association (www.americanhumane.org), Rape, Abuse, and Incest National Network (www.rainn.org), The Family Violence Prevention Fund (www.fvpf.org), Depression.com (www.depression.com), or Christians In Recovery (www.christians-in-recovery.com).

LETHAL LIES

1. What was the **worst** thing that happened to you because you lied?

2. Check out these verses from Psalms. What do they say will happen to liars?
   Psalm 5:6
   Psalm 5:10
   Psalm 12:2-3

3. Read **Psalm 109:1-5**. What bad attitudes and unfair actions do you see in the liars that attacked David?

4. What did David do when these liars slandered him? Take a look at one of these verses, then rewrite it in your own words.

   Psalm 5:2   Psalm 109:4   Psalm 109:30-31
   Psalm 5:7   Psalm 109:28

5. Your friend has bluntly lied to your face (or told a lie about you) and you've found out about it. What could happen in this situation if you—

   Ignored the lie and tried to forget about it?

   Got revenge and told a lie about your friend?

   Cussed your friend out?

   Told your friend you forgave them?

   Prayed for this friend?

6. Check out **Ephesians 4:25, 29**. What do you think these verses say about telling the truth?

LETHAL LIES [slander—Psalm 5, 12, 109]

THIS WEEK

Everyone knows that it's wrong to lie—and it's no fun to be lied to. This TalkSheet will foster an open discussion on lying, being the target of lies, and what God says about it all.

OPENER

For this activity you'll need three index cards—on an card write, "Give a false answer to every question, but try to make your lies sound believable." On another write, "Give a truthful answer to every question." On a third card write, "Lie on the first three questions; tell the truth on the rest. Try to make your lies sound believable." Pick three volunteers to sit at the front of the room, and give each volunteer one of the cards, instructing them to do as it says.

Then ask the following questions of each volunteer, allowing each to answer the first question before going on to the second, and so on.
⇨ Are you related to a famous person? If so, who?
⇨ Have you ever won anything worth more than $100? If so, what was it?
⇨ What is your favorite hobby?
⇨ Where is the most interesting place you've ever been?
⇨ What is your favorite color?
⇨ Have you ever been mentioned in a newspaper or on TV? If so, what was the reason?

After your volunteers have answered, reveal which contestant was always telling the truth, which was always lying, and which did both. Your group can then check their charts for accuracy. The student who was the best at distinguishing lies from the truth wins.

THE DISCUSSION, BY NUMBERS

1. Let some of your group members share their experiences. What were the consequences of their lies? How did these situations turn out? Point out that the negative consequences of lies outweigh any positive benefits.

2. What did these verses say about lying? What are the Biblical consequences of lying? How does this apply to the lives of your kids today?

3. Take some time to talk about the characteristics of the people who lied to King David. You may want to make a list of these for the group to see. How do these liars relate to the liars in the lives of your kids?

4. Break your group into pairs or groups of three and assign a passage to each group. Help students to understand David's response to the liars. He prayed for them, did good to them, and showed them friendship. Though David expressed his desire to see these liars come to ruin, it's important to note that David never tried to bring that about himself. Instead, he turned it over to God to handle.

5. The purpose of this is to discuss the different approaches to handling lying. Each reaction could bring a different result. Talk about each response and the pros and cons of each one. In your kids' opinions, what is the best way to handle a situation like this?

6. Point out that Ephesians 4:25 speaks about replacing the negative (lying) with the positive (telling the truth). In essence, Paul is telling people how to get rid of a bad habit—don't just stop it, replace it with something godly. Verse 29 tells people to replace any unwholesome speech (lies, gossip, berating) with words that encourage and build up another person.

THE CLOSE

Every one of your students has been the victim of a lie, in some form or another. Question 4 explains how to handle it. What can your kids do if they hear a lie about someone else?

What difference can your kids make through their actions today? Ask them to take a look at their lives. How would they rate themselves on a scale of 1-10 (1 being "I'm a true liar", 10 being "I'm 100% honest")? Challenge them to change their approach to lying and see how it affects themselves and their relationships with others.

MORE

● In consideration with this discussion, how does lying affect relationships with others? How has the media portrayed lying? What myths have been formed about lying from commercials, TV shows, or movies? How have on-line chat rooms and Web pages made it easy to disguise oneself and lie about others? What other examples of slander and lying have your kids seen in the media and in society today? And how does this apply to the psalm that you've discussed?

● Too often people aren't praised for being honest and trustworthy. Challenge your kids to thank their friends and family members for being honest with them. Encouragement makes people feel good! Encourage your kids and thank them for being honest with you. Imagine how God feels when he sees people upholding the truth!

PRECIOUS TO GOD!

1. How much **value** do you think you have (not your possessions, but who you are)? Rank yourself on the scale below.

◆ ▌▌▌▌▌▌▌▌▌▌▌▌▌▌▌▌▌▌▌▌▌▌▌ ◆

No value whatsoever   I'm priceless

2. Check out **Psalm 8**. What question does David asks in verse 4?

David then lists some things God has done to show how much he values people (verses 5-8). Which one is your favorite?

3. Now turn to and read **John 3:16**. Because of his great love for people, what did God do?

What does this tell you about how God values you?

4. Check out **Romans 8:31-32**, then use the scale below to rate how much you think God values you.

Not at all   Some   A lot   Wow, he loves me how much?

5. What is **one word** that describes how you feel knowing that God will always love you?

PRECIOUS TO GOD! [God's love for people—Psalm 8]

THIS WEEK

God values each of your kids so highly. This may be hard for teenagers to understand—most junior highers struggle with self-esteem. They can't image someone loving them completely for who they are. On top of that, some of your kids may struggle from feeling unloved by parents, ditched by friends, and unappreciated by others. Use this TalkSheets to point out that value that comes from God, and not from themselves. That's what makes their lives worthwhile and meaningful!

OPENER

Show your students a dollar bill or a dollar coin and ask your kids why they think it's valuable. Point out that the dollar is just paper (or a simple coin!)—not very valuable in and of itself. You may want to describe or show pictures of other things that have no real value other than what people attach to them—a famous painting, an expensive baseball card, a rare CD, and so on. Point out that many things are valuable only because people have decided to attach value to them. The world's most expensive painting, for instance, would be of no value at all say, to monkey or a pet cat. Why do your kids think they're valuable? Who has attached value to them?

THE DISCUSSION, BY NUMBERS

1. How did your kids rank themselves? This will be a good indicator of their self-esteems. Be careful not to ask for specific rankings, as they may not want to share their personal feelings about themselves. Instead, ask them how junior highers in general would rank themselves.

2. What question did David ask in verse 4? Have your kids ever asked the same question? You may want to ask your group to rephrase David's question in everyday language. Knowing that God has done a lot of awesome things for them, which one is the favorite of your kids? Why?

3. By now your students should be convinced that God values them highly. Read Romans 5:8 to your group and point out that Christ died for people even while people were yet sinners. That is, he loved people even when people were in total rebellion against him! How many of your kids would've done that if they were Jesus?

4. In question 1, your kids ranked themselves. How do they think God values them? Point out that God's love is based on his nature—not on how popular, cute, talented, rich, or funny people are. His love is unconditional, never-ending, and always the same. All of your kids should put themselves at the highest end of this scale.

5. You may make a list of the words that they chose, knowing that God loves them all the time, no matter what. Ask for a few volunteers to explain why they chose the reaction they did. Did any of them respond negatively? Some of them may have a hard time understanding the concept of God's love. Take some time to talk about these reactions, too.

THE CLOSE

Take a moment to affirm your appreciation and love for your students. Point out that each of them is extremely valuable to the group and that you the different characteristics that they bring to the group. The uniqueness of your kids brings variety to the group. You may want to illustrate this by using some colored markers. Pick a color (say, red) and say that red stands for humor. Blue for loyalty, green for enthusiasm, and so on. Each of your kids brings color and wholeness to the group—as they do to the family of God! Without that variety, a group would be dull. Close with a time of prayer for your group and for each person in it.

MORE

● You may want to brainstorm with your kids practical ways that your kids show their value for someone else—a friend, family member, teacher, pastor, and so on. What could your kids do this week for someone that they appreciate? Encourage them to follow through with it—it may be a simple e-mail, note, or phone call. Did this action change the relationship in any way? How did the other person respond?

● How does the media and society shape what people value? You may want to spend some time talking with your kids about how TV, movies, and music have affected what others think of each other. For example, what do movies say about sexual respect and genuine love? Who does society hold in high esteem? And is that person worthy of ultimate respect and admiration? How do these influences compare to your kids' individual admirations and high regard for others? What about Christians at large?

IS GOD KEEPING SCORE?

1. Have any of these things occurred in your school or neighborhood?
   Stealing
   Drug dealing
   Fistfighting
   Shooting
   Cheating in class
   Vandalism
   Sexual harassment
   Violence against a teacher
   Gang fights

2. Check out what **Psalm 10** has to say about evil people. How are they described in this psalm and what awaits them when God steps in?

3. Now take a look at **2 Corinthians 1:3-4**.

   What does God do for people in their troubles?

   What does this passage say people can do for others?

4. A friend of yours has become a victim of violence at school. Based on what you read in 2 Corinthians 1:3-4, how would you respond to the following questions?

   As a Christian, what could you say or do to help your friend come through this situation?

   What if your friend asked why God didn't step in and stop the violence that injured them?

   What have you learned from Psalm 10 that would help you come up with a response?

5. Why do you think it's a good thing to turn to God for comfort?

IS GOD KEEPING SCORE? [unfair world—Psalm 10]

THIS WEEK

This TalkSheet deals with the rough times when bad people seem to get away with harmful things—and when God seems slow to respond. Your students will see that God moves at his own perfect speed and no injustice will go unpunished. They'll also have the opportunity to discuss ways they can help comfort hurting people.

OPENER

You may want to show a few current newspaper headlines, featuring harmful or violent crimes that people have committed. Ask your group a question like, "Why do you suppose God lets people get away with stuff like this—or does he? What do you think?"

What about your kids lives? Is there stuff going on in their lives that they don't understand—that doesn't seem fair? Depending on your group, you may want to open this how you feel is the most appropriate for discussion.

THE DISCUSSION, BY NUMBERS

1. Some of these things have undoubtedly happened in your students' schools and neighborhoods. Did any of the people get away with these actions? Were they caught—and if so, did they get off lightly? You may want to mention that the author of Psalm 10 (probably David) also wondered why people who did bad things sometimes seemed to get off scot-free.

2. You may want to read the psalm to the group, or have volunteers read portions. The psalm talks about the ultimate victory that God has over evil and injustice. How might this psalm offer comfort to the victims of any of the incidents described earlier?

3. What do these verses say about injustices? Help your kids understand that one of the reasons Christians experience unfair problems may be to prepare them to comfort and help others in similar circumstances.

4. Based on the question 3, how would your kids respond to these questions? Take some time to talk about each one and discuss the reactions that your kids have. Have any of them encountered a situation like this? Are any of them feeling this way right now?

5. However your group responded the fact remains that God does care. He takes wicked people into account and will thoroughly punish evildoers. Psalm 10 promises these things to all of people. God may seem very far away from some of your kids. You may want to ask them to describe how close they feel to God. If they don't understand that he cares—or can't feel it—challenge them to spend ten minutes each day this week with God. They can just sit and think about him, vent about their problems to him, whatever. They may just find that he's not too far away.

THE CLOSE

Everyone gets hurt unjustly in some way or another. That's the tragedy of sin. But God has turned that hurt into a positive thing—the ability to sympathize with and comfort another suffering person. You may want to review the principles of Psalm 10 again with your kids. God comforts the victims who commit themselves to his loving care. You may want to read these promises about God's paybacks—Romans 12:19; Hebrews 10:30-31; and 2 Peter 3:8-9. What hope do your kids find in these verses? How can they apply these promises to their lives today? If they rewrote on of these verses in their own words, what would it say?

MORE

- You may want to videotape one or more segments of the local or network TV news that show violent, harmful, or unfair things happening to innocent victims (be sure to screen them!). Watch the clips with your students and discuss various things Christians could have done—or could do now— to help justice be served. Could your students lend a hand in righting a wrong they see on the tape? If so, how?

- Although kids can get hurt, some of your group members may be dealing with larger issues in their lives—such as sexual abuse, suicide, divorce, depression, or some other issue. If you sense this, you may want to take some time to talk about these. Be sensitive to your group members and encourage them to find a trusted adult (including you) to talk with. For more information, visit the Rape, Abuse, and Incest National Network (www.rainn.org) or National Coalition Against Sexual Assault (http://ncasa.org), the National Council on Alcoholism and Drug Dependence, Inc. (http://ncadd.org) or the Addiction Research Foundation (www.arf.org/isd/info.html), Suicide Voices Awareness of Education (www.save.org), the National Foundation For Depressive Illness, Inc. (www.depression.org), or the Youth Specialties Web page (www.YouthSpecialties.com) for links to information and resources.

BEING A FOOL

1. Rank the following actions from the **most foolish (1)** to the **least foolish (15)**.

____ Cussing out a classmate
____ Going too far sexually
____ Skipping team practice
____ Ignoring your parents' rules
____ Cutting class
____ Smoking cigarettes
____ Hitting a sibling
____ Trying to be something you're not
____ Not obeying God

____ Spending too much money
____ Ditching your boyfriend or girlfriend
____ Forgetting your lunch money
____ Getting involved in a fight with a gang member
____ Lying to your teacher
____ Cheating on a test

2. Check out **Psalm 14**. What does **verse 1** say is inside a fool's heart (who they really are)?

What does **verse 2** say about the contents of a fool's head (do they understand God)?

What does **verse 3** say about the direction fools point their feet (in which direction are they going)?

3. Read what the foolish man did in **Matthew 7:26-27**. Would that be the same as ignoring Jesus' words? Why or why not?

4. Take a look at the following Bible verses to see some of the things a fool does. Draw a line from each passage on the left to the matching characteristic on the right.

Proverbs 10:8	Fools show everyone how stupid they are.
Proverbs 10:18	Fools talk too much and come to ruin.
Proverbs 10:23	Fools are reckless.
Proverbs 12:15	Fools enjoy evil conduct.
Proverbs 12:16	Fools waste money.
Proverbs 14:1	Fools never admit they are wrong.
Proverbs 14:9	Fools live self-destructive lives.
Proverbs 14:16	Fools are hot-tempered.
Proverbs 15:5	Fools spread slander (untrue gossip).
Proverbs 17:16	Fools ignore parental discipline.
Proverbs 18:2	Fools don't take care of their own lives.
Proverbs 21:20	Fools don't save or plan for the future.
Ecclesiastes 4:5	Fools like to blab their own uninformed opinions.
Ecclesiastes 10:3	Fools won't listen to advice.

BEING A FOOL [foolishness—Psalm 14]

THIS WEEK

No kid wants to be a fool. But the way they define a fool is different from the way God defines it. To teens a fool is a nerd, a thief who gets caught, a loser, or an ugly dresser. To God a fool is someone who ignores him. This TalkSheet will give your kids insights into how not to be a fool in God's eyes.

OPENER

One at a time, hold up some of the following objects so everyone can see—a $20 bill, a toothbrush and toothpaste, and a picture of a stop sign or speed limit sign, and so on. If your group members were the biggest fools on earth, how would they treat or respond to the objects you displayed? They'll probably say to ignore or mishandle things like money, hygiene, and safety. Tell the group that there is one other thing that fools stupidly ignore (which is God, but don't tell them that!). Then launch into the discussion.

THE DISCUSSION, BY NUMBERS

1. How did your kids rank these items? Some of these items result in serious consequences. You may want to make a master list of their rankings. Where did "not obeying God" rank with your kids? Point out that disobeying God not only affects their life on earth, but life in eternity too.

2. The passage tells people that a fool's heart is filled with unbelief, his head is filled with lack of understanding, and his feet are taking him away from God. Discuss the meaning of each answer. The third verse might get your kids thinking—they may question God's statement that there's no one who does good. After asking for their opinions remind the group that God's definition of a good person is someone equal in goodness and sinlessness to his son, Jesus Christ.

3. Discuss the imagery that Jesus used—the lack of surefootedness, the pressures, and the failure. Make sure students note that it isn't just hearing Christ's words but obeying them that makes the difference.

4. This activity covers a lot of passages. If you need to keep this exercise short, assign verses to volunteer readers and let the group pick the match. You may want to also discuss whether or not these are common problems among teens. Would a person who behaved in these ways be considered a fool by most teens? What is the opposite of each foolish action? Do your students know people who set positive examples by doing the positive things?

THE CLOSE

Point out that the only way not to be a fool in God's eyes is to open up to him, read the Bible, and do what it says. The core of foolishness is ignoring God, which turns into disobeying God. Encourage your kids to get to know God better in a reasonable way—maybe start by reading a verse a day, praying for a few minutes each day, or writing in a student journal (be sure to set tangible goals that they can follow through with). You may want to provide or recommend resources for your kids—devotional Bibles and student journals to help your kids get in sync with God. For more information, check out the resources at www.YouthSpecialties.com or www.zondervan.com, including the Wild Truth series for junior highers and the *Teen Devotional Bible* (Zondervan).

MORE

● You may want to make a two-column list on a whiteboard or poster board of God's fools and world's fools. Ask your kids to come up with a list under each item of how a Christian can be a fool for God. Then come up with a list of actions or items for how a person is a fool for the world. How do the two compare? Which items or actions overlap? Which don't? And how can a person find a balance?

● How does the media portray foolishness? The media's definition of foolishness is drastically different than God's. Ask your kids what they think. What TV show or movie characters are portrayed as fools? What does a fool do or say? And how do others respond to him? You may want to show a few clips from a TV show or movie (be sure to screen them!) and talk about any foolish actions or characteristics that are shown.

NOT SHAKEN

1. Imagine three people—a star athlete, a supermodel, and a music legend. In the list of talents and traits below, put an **A** next to all those that would make an **athlete** a star. Do the same for a **model (M)** and a **music legend (L)**. Some traits may get more than one initial—some may have none.

___ Lots of friends
___ Fabulous singing voice
___ Trendy clothes
___ Knock 'em dead good looks
___ Super intelligence
___ Bulging muscles
___ Straight, white teeth
___ Good coordination
___ Creativity
___ Highly paid agent

___ Shiny, healthy hair
___ Perfect body
___ Cool parents
___ Solid stage presence
___ Strong bones
___ Clear skin
___ Plenty of money
___ Loud voice
___ Photogenic looks
___ Remarkable stamina

2. Now put a **C** next to all the above traits you think would make a **Christian** a superstar in God's eyes.

3. Check out **Psalm 15**, where the psalmist lists the traits that God looks for in people. List the traits mentioned in the following verses.
   Verse 2—
   Verse 3—
   Verse 4—
   Verse 5—

4. Is it possible for the supermodel, star athlete, and music legend to have none of the traits mentioned in Psalm 15 and still be super-successful in their line of work?
   How?

   Is it possible for a Christian to have none of these traits and be a godly person?
   How?

5. Put a check mark by the two godly traits from question 3 that you think you're doing well at. Then put an arrow by two others you think you need to work at the most.

NOT SHAKEN [godliness—Psalm 15]

THIS WEEK

Sports heroes, music legends, supermodels—are these people real winners? God has a different definition. A good example of what he calls a winner is given in Psalm 15. This TalkSheet provides you with an opportunity to set some young lives on the right path to real success.

OPENER

Offer a simple prize (dollar bill, candy bar, soda, gift certificate, and so on) to the student who can come the closest to guessing anything you choose—it can be your weight, age, family placement, or some other fact about yourself, or facts about your church, city, or someone else in your group. When you've determined the winner, make a show of praising this person's wonderful winning ways and (tongue-in-cheek) make everyone else aware that they are losers. Then explain that, in order for someone to win, someone else must lose. Ask your students to think of situations where there are losers as well as winners (sports, contests, job opportunities, and the like). How did these situations make them feel? How do others react to losing? Point out that their ideas of winning are often not the same as God's and the TalkSheet will help them sort out the differences.

THE DISCUSSION, BY NUMBERS

1. Discuss students' answers, then ask them to name famous winners in any field, not just the ones listed. Do these winners have the traits listed? It's likely that no one will mention a Bible character. What biblical character would they consider to be a superstar?

2. God has a list of traits that he admires in people, but they are considerably different than those listed in question 1 (which don't match the godly characteristics of Psalm 15). Take some time to talk about the characteristics that your group thinks God values in people. You may want to make a list of their thoughts on a poster board or whiteboard.

3. This is a follow up to number 2. Check out the traits that your kids listed. They'll probably wonder about verse 4, which speaks of despising a vile man. Point out that this means a strong refusal to be in partnership with the sins of others. As you discuss each trait, ask your kids to define them their own words. How do these traits apply to their lives today?

4. Give your kids some time to think this through and respond. You might want to reiterate that the traits at the top of the page are very different from the godly traits. Which set of traits would tend to last a whole lifetime and which set tends to disappear with age? Which set is mostly outside appearance and which set comes from the inside of a person? Which set is based on natural talents that people are born with, and which set can anyone acquire with God's help?

5. Give volunteers an opportunity to tell which traits they would like to develop. How can they being to develop these traits today?

THE CLOSE

Point out that nobody—no Christian—is perfect. The only person who exhibited the all these traits was Jesus. Take some time to talk about what traits your kids would like to work on in their lives. What makes this easy or difficult? You may want to write these traits on pieces of paper (you'll need multiple papers for each trait, depending on the size of your group) and let your kids pick one. Ask them to take a few minutes to consider how well they demonstrate that characteristic. Do they need to work on this trait? If so, how?

MORE

● You might want to ask your kids to find some articles about famous people in magazine, on the Internet, or in the tabloids. The articles should feature photographs of the celebrities—some of which talk their unhappiness or what sinful things they've been up to. Some of these articles aren't true, but the pictures and stories make people believe the false stories. How believeable are the stories to your kids? Why? How do the traits portrayed by the person in these stories compare to those in Psalm 15?

● Not all celebrities, movie stars, stellar athletes, and music legends are ungodly or unworthy of respect. In fact some of these people are fine examples of how to live good lives. You may want to brainstorm some of these people with your group. Are any of these Christians? Do their lifestyles show it and if so, are they vocal about their faith? Use this activity to illustrate that fame isn't bad—but how people handle their beliefs and lifestyles is.

COUNT YOUR BLESSINGS

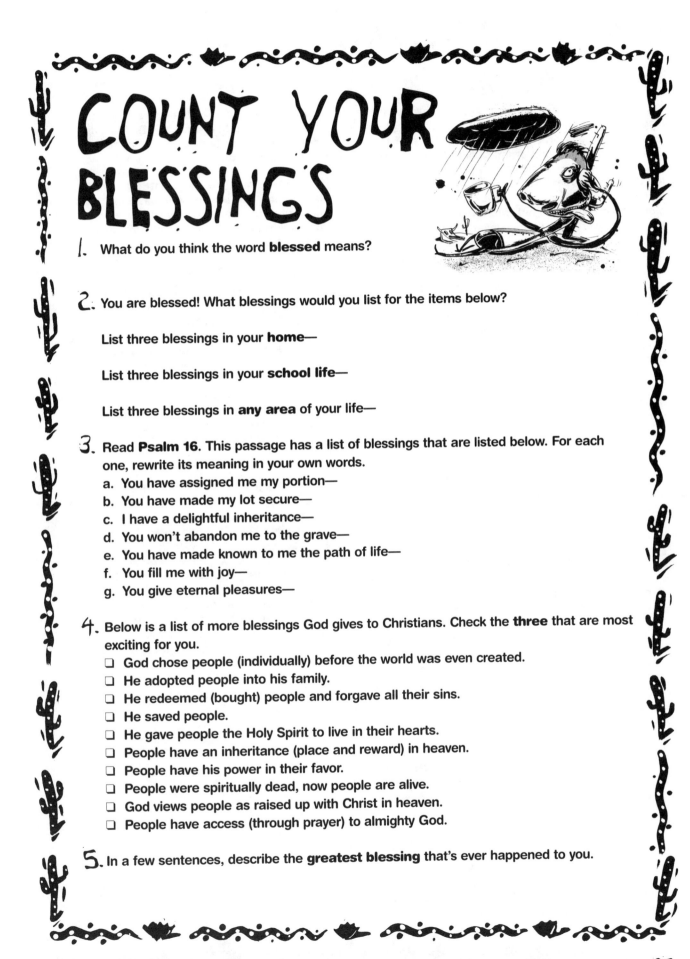

1. What do you think the word **blessed** means?

2. You are blessed! What blessings would you list for the items below?

   List three blessings in your **home**—

   List three blessings in your **school life**—

   List three blessings in **any area** of your life—

3. Read **Psalm 16**. This passage has a list of blessings that are listed below. For each one, rewrite its meaning in your own words.
   a. You have assigned me my portion—
   b. You have made my lot secure—
   c. I have a delightful inheritance—
   d. You won't abandon me to the grave—
   e. You have made known to me the path of life—
   f. You fill me with joy—
   g. You give eternal pleasures—

4. Below is a list of more blessings God gives to Christians. Check the **three** that are most exciting for you.
   ❏ God chose people (individually) before the world was even created.
   ❏ He adopted people into his family.
   ❏ He redeemed (bought) people and forgave all their sins.
   ❏ He saved people.
   ❏ He gave people the Holy Spirit to live in their hearts.
   ❏ People have an inheritance (place and reward) in heaven.
   ❏ People have his power in their favor.
   ❏ People were spiritually dead, now people are alive.
   ❏ God views people as raised up with Christ in heaven.
   ❏ People have access (through prayer) to almighty God.

5. In a few sentences, describe the **greatest blessing** that's ever happened to you.

COUNT YOUR BLESSINGS [being blessed—Psalm 16]

THIS WEEK

This TalkSheet discusses the blessings of knowing Christ and why your kids can say, "My heart is glad and my tongue rejoices" (Psalm 16:9). But life has times when it's difficult or impossible to feel blessed and happy—maybe some of your kids are experiencing this. Do be sensitive to your kids through this discussion. For discussion items on abuse, depression, and more, check out these TalkSheets—Is God Keeping Score? (19), Divine Desert (59) or Core for Living (65).

OPENER

You may want to start by having your kids share or tell about some experiences or times in their lives when they felt like King David in Psalm 16:9. When did your kids feel their heart filled with joy and their tongue expressed happiness and praise? Take a few minutes to talk about what times make your kids the most happy. What about these times make your kids feel content and filled with joy? And when they felt this happiness and joy, did they give God the honor and praise him? Why or why not?

THE DISCUSSION, BY NUMBERS

1. You may want to make a master list of your kids' answers. Point out that the Bible defines blessed as happy and to be envied. Christians are in an enviable position because of their relationship with God.

2. You're kids will come up with all kinds of blessings. You may want to list these as well. Point out how much they've been given—homes, friends, church, school, food everyday, fresh water, and so on. Ask them to think of the tiniest blessings that others don't have. For example, what do your kids have that a person in a third world country may not have? As the discussion progresses, remind everyone of two things—God is the source of all good blessings and people should have a thankful attitude for the things he gives them.

3. How did your kids reword these blessings? Take some time to talk about each blessing. Point out that Psalm 16 is just a small sample of the many Bible passages that speak of the awesome gifts Christians can enjoy. What are some other blessings that are listed in the Bible?

4. Ask your students to explain which blessings they chose and why they chose the ones they did. Be sure that everyone understands each statement and what blessing is included. Which blessing would your group consider to be the absolute best? Why? If you have time, you may want to have your students explore the Bible to find where these blessings can be found (check out book of Ephesians!).

5. If you have time, you may want to let some kids share their experiences. You may want to let your kids write their greatest blessings on a sheet of large white paper or newsprint. Provide markers for your kids to use.

THE CLOSE

Thanking God isn't just for Thanksgiving Day! God loves it when people praise him and thank him for what he's given people! After all, doesn't it feel good to be thanked after you've done something? Ask your kids to think how they feel when they never get thanked for anything they've done or given someone else.

Close in a time of prayer, either with the group or individually, for your kids to thank God for everything God has given them. Challenge them to thank God for at least one blessing each day.

MORE

● Do your kids like hands-on activities? Collect a stack of magazines from which your students can clip photos, headlines, and drawings that illustrate the blessings that God has given them. You'll need some glue, glue sticks, or rolls of tape. Then let your kids make a giant collage on a large piece of roll-out white paper or poster boards.

● Thanksgiving dinner anyone? Well, maybe not a full-blown Thanksgiving, but you may want to do something fun with your kids, like hold a mini-Thanksgiving dinner or dessert night. Use this time to reflect with your kids on what they are thankful for and how God has blessed them.

BRING IT ON!

1. List two of your **most important** personal goals.

2. Check out **Psalm 20** and then match the phrases on the left with the correct endings on the right.

May the Lord answer you when—	plans succeed.
May his name—	sacrifices.
May he send you—	support.
May he grant you—	burnt offerings.
May he remember all your—	the desire of your heart.
May he accept your—	you are in distress.
May he give you—	protect you.
May he make all your—	help.
May he grant all your—	requests.

3. Check out these situations below and answer the questions under each one.

   a. Sophia wants to finish school with high honors, and she knows she has to work hard.
   - What are three things she must do to achieve it?

   - What are three things she must *not* do to achieve it?

   - How can God help?

   b. Monte wants to be a track star, but he's not sure he has the discipline.
   - What are three things he must do to achieve it?

   - What are three things he must *not* do to achieve it?

   - How can God help?

   c. Delisa wants to stay away from alcohol, but her mom's an alcoholic.
   - What are three things she must do to achieve it?

   - What are three things she must *not* do to achieve it?

   - How can God help?

4. Check out **Psalm 20:7-8**. What message is God sending to you in these verses?

BRING IT ON! [facing challenges—Psalm 20]

THIS WEEK

Young people face significant challenges in their daily lives. Some challenges are in the area of temptations, like resisting drugs, staying sexually pure, and dealing with anger or depression. Other challenges are more positive, such as striving to do well in school, succeeding in athletics, or reaching personal goals. In Psalm 20 David prayed for victory in battle. His prayer shows teens that the best way to face any challenge is at the side of God. This TalkSheet gives your group a chance to see how God's power can help anyone meet life's challenges.

OPENER

You may want to take this opportunity to tell your class about a difficult challenge you faced—or read a story by someone who did face a challenge. Tell how God helped you (or the person) through it—or if you weren't a Christian how you think God could have played a greater part in your struggle. Let your kids ask you questions about the situation and your faith.

Or present a challenge to your kids. Have them make a list of the three most difficult challenges that they face. Write these challenges down. Now ask them how they or their peers deal with these challenges. What are the different ways to handle these and what are the most effective ways? How do most teenagers their age deal with their problems? Why?

THE DISCUSSION, BY NUMBERS

1. Because some of these goals may be personal, let the students know that don't have to share their thoughts with the group. Some students will be willing to talk about personal goals. Ask about some of the steps required to meet the goal, which are the hardest steps, and what might they have to give up in order to meet the goal.

2. Talk about each of these phrases with the group. You may want to have them re-phrase the statements in their own words and explain how the statements apply to their lives. Which one of these is most encouraging to your kids? Why?

3. You may want to split your group into smaller groups to discuss these situations. Talk about each situation and how each person could—or could not—achieve their goals. Point out that God can help! For example, he could help Sophia achieve her educational goals by giving her the energy she needs to study late, giving her a clear mind and a good memory, and by helping her answer test questions with just the right words.

The Lord could give Monte a committed coach who could help him to stick to his practice program. God could help Delisa realize that she needs to find non-drinking friends who support her.

4. How did your kids re-phrase these verses? What does this mean to your kids in their lives today?

THE CLOSE

Start off by hanging a large piece of roll-out paper or a whiteboard on the wall. Provide several different colored pens or markers. On the top, in big letters, print VICTORY. Under that, print the phrase GOD, HELP US (OR ME) TO— Then give each student a chance to jot a short end to that sentence. Urge everyone to write a goal that they think God can help them reach. Then look over these goals with the group. How would they like to start to reach those goals today? What questions do they have? Where can they go to get the encouragement that they need?

MORE

- You may want to encourage your group to form a support or encouragement network. What are the goals that your kids have? How can they help each other reach these goals? Maybe your kids want to have an e-mail prayer request list or construct their own Web page. How can God use fellow believers to encourage and support them?

- Take a look at Psalm 20: "Some trust in chariots and some in horses but people trust in the name of the Lord their God." Back in King David's day, chariots and horses meant safety, wealth, or power. What do people today trust in, instead of chariots and horses? You may want to rewrite your own verse 7 with your group to say something like "Some trust in money and some in fame but people trust in the name of the Lord their God."

FOLLOWING THE LEADER

1. Try to remember a time when you were a kid when you got lost or separated from your parent. Circle the **two words** that describe how you felt.

Unconcerned	Shocked	Dismayed
Panicked	Worried	Confused
Curious	Terrified	Sad
Fearful	Confident	Alarmed
Abandoned	Relaxed	
Dumb	Unafraid	

2. If you were to go anyplace in the world to explore, where would you go?

   Would you want a **guide** with you?

   Why or why not?

3. Do you think people need a guide to get them through life? Why or why not?

4. Check out **Psalm 23** and complete the phrase in your own words from what the Bible says.
   He is the shepherd—
   He makes me—
   He leads me—
   He guides me—
   He is with me—
   His rod and staff—
   He prepares—
   He anoints my head—

5. From what you've read in Psalm 23, how would you describe the condition of a person if God was **not** a shepherd and guide.

6. Who do you think guides **you** the most through life?
   - ❏ My friends
   - ❏ My parents
   - ❏ A teacher
   - ❏ My boyfriend or girlfriend
   - ❏ A little of everyone
   - ❏ Myself
   - ❏ My youth pastor
   - ❏ Another relative
   - ❏ Another relative
   - ❏ God
   - ❏ I have no guide
   - ❏ Other—

FOLLOWING THE LEADER [following Christ—Psalm 23]

THIS WEEK

Life is a journey and those who've been on the path long enough realize that it's full of pitfalls and dark passages. This journey is a serious and potentially disastrous the trip that requires a guide—someone who knows every turn, every safe resting place, every refreshing stream. Psalm 23 paints a picture of the care and guidance that each of people needs. Submitting to the leading of God is an act of wisdom and personal safety.

OPENER

Introduce this topic by emphasizing the importance of having a leader or guide. You may want to go with your kids to a place that they don't know and are very unfamiliar with. (Of course, alert their parents and your church leaders of the plan first.) Maybe take them to a house in a nearby place they're unfamiliar with (this is easy to do with junior highers, because they can't drive yet). If you do this activity with a large group, you may want to split your kids into small groups—but be sure that there's an adult leader (who knows what's going on) with each group. Don't give your kids a map. They can't ask the adult leader for help or guidance—no phone calls either. They must either find their way to a specific spot or figure out how to get home from there. Later, have your leaders drive the kids back to a central meeting spot and debrief on the activity. How did your kids feel knowing that they had no idea where they were or how they were going to get home? What did they do to find the answers? Did they feel alone or stranded? Use this intro to jump into your TalkSheet discussion on Christ as the leader.

THE DISCUSSION, BY NUMBERS

1. Have a few student volunteers describe their experiences, sharing how they felt and any lessons that they learned. What was their first reaction? How long did they feel this way?

2. Point out that there are some places on earth where most of people would really want to have an experienced guide traveling with people—the Sahara desert, Mount Everest, or the Amazon jungle. Where would your kids go and would they want a guide? Why or why not?

3. Discuss the need for a guide in the lives of your kids. Why do your kids think a guide would be important or necessary? If so, in which areas of their lives—only some, or all of their lives? Have your group brainstorm the qualities that would make the ideal guide, and list those qualities on a whiteboard.

4. After your students have completed the sentences in their own words, ask them to explain how these verses apply to their lives today. For example, what is a "green pasture" to your kids?

5. What would a person's life be like with out God as guide? What would be different about their lives than the lives of a Christian? What are some other guides that people turn to in their lives? Why?

6. Ask your students to honestly consider who or what guides them through life—a parent? Boyfriend or girlfriend? The desire to have things? Talk about the wisdom of making God the only voice people listen to for advice on the path of life.

THE CLOSE

Reemphasize the idea that everyone is a stranger to life—no one knows the road ahead. Encourage your kids to make Christ their guide now—he can help them and get them through the pits, dead ends, and unknown trails that abound in life. Explain how God guides them with his word and comforts them with the Holy Spirit. What better leader could they ask for?

MORE

● Psalm 23 is often recited at funerals or in times of pain and sorrow. Point out that although verse 4 is a great comfort, the whole psalm is extremely valuable to their lives. You may want to split this psalm by verse and have small groups take a closer look at the verse. What does each verse say to your kids and those their same age? Encourage your kids to rewrite the verse in their own words and then construct the group's version of the psalm when they've finished in their groups.

● You may want to ask your kids to think about the analogy of God as the shepherd and people as the sheep. What characteristics of sheep do humans have in this analogy? Point out that sheep are completely dependent on the shepherd for provision, guidance, and protection. With God as the shepherd, people are his sheep—not frightened, passive animals, but obedient followers. In this context, the sheep are wise enough to follow the one who will lead them in the right places and in right ways

THE PERFECT PARENT

1. List the **three** of the **best times** you ever had with your parents or guardians.

   List the **three** of the **worst times**.

2. What do you think—**A (all the time)**, **S (sometimes)**, **W (when they want to)**, or **N (never)**?
   ___ My parent(s) trust me.
   ___ My parent(s) listen to me.
   ___ My parent(s) mistreat me.
   ___ My parents are separated or divorced.
   ___ My parent(s) abuse me.
   ___ My parent(s) have a bad habit.
   ___ My parent(s) respect me.
   ___ My parent(s) love me.

3. Do you agree with this statement?
   If you have bad parents, there's nothing you can do about it.

4. Check out **Psalm 27:10** and answer the questions below.

   How do you think God feels about you?

   What do you think he'll do because of his feelings?

   What won't he do?

   Is he likely to change his feelings?

   Why or why not?

5. These verses say some things about **parents**. Read each verse and finish the statement in your own words.
   Deuteronomy 5:16   I do this by—
   Ephesians 6:1   I do this by—
   Proverbs 1:8-9   I do this. The last thing they taught me is—

THE PERFECT PARENT [parents—Psalm 27]

THIS WEEK

For the first time in America, single-parent families outnumber two-parent families. Even teens with two parents often deal with a stepparent or a mom or dad who is alcoholic, abusive, or distant. Note: The term parent here and in the following items refers to all kinds of parenting adults—birth, step, foster, or guardian. Be sensitive to the fact that there's a good chance your kids aren't in a traditional family and may be hurting.

This TalkSheet points out that God loves each and every teen. He can fill the void and soothe the pain. And it will allow discussion on ways to deal with difficult family situations.

OPENER

Work together as a group to come up with a classified ad for the ideal, perfect parent(s). Your teens may suggest things like money or a cool house, but try to steer them toward character traits such as loyalty, compassion, and so on. If any of your kids mention that they have good parents, ask them share some of the things that make their parents successful. But be sensitive to the kids in your group who may not have the ideal parents.

Jot the ad on the whiteboard or a large piece of paper. You may want to comment that perfect parents are hard to find. Almost everyone has trouble with their mom or dad sooner or later. But do your kids know that they do have a perfect parent waiting for them in heaven and listening to their every need?

THE DISCUSSION, BY NUMBERS

1. Your kids may have different responses. Let your kids share a few of their answers. Some of these troubles may not be self-inflicted like alcoholism or desertion, but they are real difficulties. How did they feel toward their parents during the good times? How about the bad times?

2. How did your kids answer these questions? Some of your maybe won't want to share their responses. Be sensitive to your group through out this item. Some of them may be dealing with some very serious situations of family abuse, alcoholism, and so on. Ask your kids if the relationships with their parents have improved, gotten worse, or stayed level over the last few years. What would be the hardest things to do well as a parent? What are some of the frustrations their parents feel?

3. Discuss what practical steps parents and their junior high or middle schoolers might need to take to solve some of the problems raised above.

What classifies a bad parent? You may want to make a list of the groups' response? For example what might lead to a better relationship in a family where the students feel they aren't listened to?

4. How did your kids answer these questions? How much do they think God loves them? Point out that if they're facing troubles with family, God is there to help. Sometimes he actually changes parents (and kids) and sometimes he provides comfort even though parents don't change. Let your kids know that you're there for them if they want to talk with someone about their parents.

5. What do these verses say about parents? Are your kids doing what the verses say? Have your class read and discuss these passages one at a time. What are some realistic ways these passages can be practiced in the family?

THE CLOSE

Parents and teenagers have struggles—they don't always get along. Some family relationships are worst than others. God offers solutions and help through these struggles, but still expects teenagers to honor, obey, and listen to their parents.

Encourage your kids to pray for their parents and family. You may want to have everyone write one or two prayer requests for themselves and their parents on slips of paper. (These requests should focus on specific problems. They can be anonymous or not.) Collect all the slips and pray for them one at a time, or redistribute them for individuals to pray.

MORE

- Pay close attention for the serious problems within your group, such as abuse or alcoholism within the home. Domestic abuse is a reality in homes today, even Christian home. For information and links to help, check out Rape, Abuse, and Incest National Network (www.rainn.org), The Family Violence Prevention Fund (www.fvpf.org), or the Youth Specialties Web page (www.YouthSpecialties.com) for further links and information.
- You may want to organize a parent appreciation event to get your parents into the meeting and interaction with your kids. Consider a fun event or simply a parent-teen dinner or dessert night. You may want to use this time to hold a panel of parents, or a discussion, about the relationships between parents and teens. What challenges do parents face? How about dealing with the teenagers? How can your kids and their parents communicate with each other better?

STANDING IN AWE

1. Circle the **two words** below that best describe your idea of God.

Savior	Creator	Enormously huge
Way too strict	Impossible to understand	Personal
Awesome	Big judge	Listens to me
Far away	Exciting	Draws me to him
Comforter	Ruler	Absent
Mysterious	Teacher	Provider
Loving	Interesting	

2. Check out **Psalm 37**. What does it say to do?

   What does it say will happen?

3. Write a sentence explaining what you think it means to **delight in the Lord**.

4. What do you think? Read each statement and answer **Y (yes)** or **N (no)**.
   ___ I'm happy that I'm a Christian
   ___ I enjoy talking to God.
   ___ I enjoy talking about God.
   ___ I want to grow more in my faith.
   ___ I can't understand everything about God.
   ___ I like these Bible studies, because I can understand them.
   ___ I can see God working in my life.
   ___ I think the idea of heaven is exciting.
   ___ I want to serve God with my life.
   ___ I'm excited about learning more about God

5. Rewrite **Psalm 37:4** in your own words, replacing the word *delight* with three phrases that describe ways to delight in God.

STANDING IN AWE [delighting in God—Psalm 37]

THIS WEEK

Youth workers teach their kids to love God by faithful acts of obedience and service, but what about the emotional aspect of love for God? Psalm 37:4 gives a short description of a heartfelt love for God—delight yourself in the Lord. This TalkSheet gives your students the opportunity to discover the joys of being delighted by God.

OPENER

Ask your group members to describe in one or two words their emotional responses to things junior high and middle schoolers like (TV shows, jelly donuts, perfect ski or surf conditions, big allowance, and so on). If your group has a favorite snack like chips and soda, you may want to serve it to them and ask how they feel about the unexpected treat. Explain that the Bible often uses a word to describe these sort of emotional feelings—delight. You can then move into the first TalkSheet activity by explaining that today's topic is delighting in (or enjoying) God.

THE DISCUSSION, BY NUMBERS

1. This helps students come to grips with their view of God. Is he exciting to them? Do they ignore him? This is a good time for you to relate your changing attitude toward God as you came to commit your life to him. Tell your class what God means to you and why.

2. Ask students to share their answers. Be sure they understand that the promise of receiving the desires of their hearts doesn't mean people can have anything people want anytime people want. The verse is saying that God will give people the object of their desires—but he'll also place his godly desires in their hearts first.

3. What does delighting in God mean to your kids? Ask for some examples and write them down on a poster board or whiteboard. Try to come up with a group consensus.

4. This activity provides your students the opportunity to evaluate their "delight factor." Encourage them to get excited about God—learning about him, thinking about him, talking to him, and so on.

5. What are some ways that your kids can delight in the Lord? How would they interpret this verse in their own lives? Make a list of their suggestions and compare them to the items in question 4.

THE CLOSE

How do your kids delight in God? Why do they love him? Ask them to think of one reason that they love God. Encourage your kids to tell God that they love him. He loves hearing praises, just like anyone does. What are they thankful for? For something different, you may want to give everyone a chance to record a message to God on videotape or state one reason why they love or appreciate God.

MORE

● You may want to talk about how to further delight in the Lord. It's great to love him and be happy with a relationship, but how can your kids get deeper into that relationship? What can they do to delight in him and learn more about him? You may want to form a small group Bible study or challenge your kids to get more involved in personal devotions. For study resources check out www.YouthSpecialties.com.

● What about those that can't delight in God—even if they want to? What if they're bogged down emotionally by too much to let go? Pay attention to those in your group who may be dealing with overwhelming circumstances, struggling at school, facing divorce or abuse at home, or some other situation. God can fill them with peace, but they may need to have someone reach out to them first.

TAKING IT WITH YOU

1. Below is a list of things you'll leave behind when your life on earth is over. Which ones will you miss the most? Rate them in order from the **you'll most hate to leave behind (1)** to those that **really won't matter (18)**

___ CD collection   ___ Church   ___ Car (if you have one)
___ Computer   ___ Vacations   ___ Money
___ TV   ___ A pet   ___ Stores
___ Your neighborhood   ___ DVD or video collection   ___ Sports
___ House   ___ Food   ___ Musical instrument
___ Video games   ___ Bedroom   ___ Other—

2. Pick one of the following passages to read and rewrite in your own words.

Psalm 49:1-9   Psalm 49:13-15

Psalm 49:10-12   Psalm 49:16-20

3. In **Luke 12:22-34**, Jesus talks about the way he cares for his creation. Draw lines to connect the things Jesus talks about with what he says about them. (Some items may match more than one phrase.)

Verse	What Jesus Speaks About	What Jesus Says About It
22-23	Food—	God clothes them in splendor.
22-23	Clothes—	Life is more than these.
24	Birds—	You are more valuable to God.
24	You—	Don't worry about it.
27	Flowers—	He knows that you need material things.
29	Your heart—	God feeds them.
30	Pagans (non-Christians)—	You must seek this.
30	Your Father—	They don't work or spin cloth.
31-32	His kingdom—	Don't set it on food or drink.
31	Things you need—	God will give you these things.
33	Treasure in heaven—	They run after material things.
		God is pleased to give it to you.
		It will never be taken from you.

4. What are four **practical things** you can do to earn rewards in heaven?

TAKING IT WITH YOU [treasures in heaven—Psalm 49]

THIS WEEK

As the bumper sticker says—No hearse tows a U-Haul. People are doomed to leave all their earthly treasures behind when they go—it makes sense to start investing in the eternal world now. This TalkSheet will provide your students with practical ways to do that.

OPENER

Ask your students to help you calculate how long it would take to drain the Pacific Ocean with an eye-dropper. The Pacific has a surface area of about 64,000,000 square miles and an average depth of about two miles. Multiply those figures to get the volume (128,000,000 cubic miles). One cubic mile equals about 150,000,000,000 cubic feet. 150,000,000,000 times 128,000,000 equals 19,200,000,000,000,000,000 cubic feet in the ocean. Multiply that times 1,728 cubic inches per cubic foot, and you have 33,177,600,000,000,000,000,000 cubic inches in the Pacific Ocean. If it takes five eyedroppers to hold a cubic inch, ask your students how many years it would take to empty the ocean at one eyedropper per second. (Round off to 30 million seconds in a year.)

Your students probably will run out of patience long before they solve the problem. Point out that emptying the ocean with an eyedropper, no matter how long it takes, is nothing compared to eternity. Each human being will live in eternity forever—it's best to plan ahead. The Bible tells people how.

THE DISCUSSION, BY NUMBERS

1. Ask students to explain their top five choices of their rankings. You may want to have the group rank them together on a whiteboard or poster board. What was most important on their list and why? Why weren't people on this list?

2. How did your kids summarize these verses? Ask for a few of them to explain what they wrote. Talk about teach verse with your group. How do these verses apply to your kids today?

3. Jesus had a lot to say in this passage. Ask for some volunteers to read the verses go through the meaning with the group. You may want to split the group into smaller groups to work on this item.

4. Your kids probably will have come up with many different ideas of what they can do. Make a master list of their ideas and ask them which ones would be the most easy from the list. Which ones would be most difficult and why? Decide on a few of them as that you could

possibly do as a group and keep this in mind for your next service project.

THE CLOSE

You've probably already covered a lot through the discussion. Close by wrapping up or answering any questions your kids may have. How do your kids think God determines what is a treasure in heaven?

MORE

● If you decide with your group to do a group project, use the checklist below to organize your students into an effective team. Have students make checklist to remind them of their commitment and duties. Be sure to get everyone's phone numbers and e-mail addresses so you can check up on them as the date nears.

    Project—
    What I need to do—
    I need to contact—
    When I'm supposed to have it done by—
    Things I need to bring—
    Other—

● For ideas on service projects and other events, check out the Ideas Library: Camps, Retreats, Missions, and Service *Ideas For Youth Groups* or the *Ideas Library on CD-ROM* (Youth Specialties).

IS HE FOR REAL?

1. Match the word in the right column that you think matches the description in the left column.

___ Agnostic   a. Isn't sure if there is a God or not

___ Atheist   b. Believes in God, but not sure which one

___ Theist   c. Believes that God doesn't exist

2. Put an arrow by the **three things** below that you think show that God does exist.

Music	Conscience	Science
Nature	Love	History
Babies	Evil	Disasters
Death	Stars in the sky	Feelings
The universe	Logic	Common sense

3. Do you **A (agree)** or **D (disagree)** with the following statements?

___ Sometimes I doubt that God really exists.

___ It would be better if God made himself more obvious.

___ God is obvious but people aren't looking or don't care.

4. Check out **Psalm 53:1-4 & 6**. In your own words describe the problems of people who say there is no God.

Who is the one who answers the prayer of verse 6?

5. There are a lot of ways people can help those who doubt God's existence. What are **three positive ways** you could explain God's existence to people, without turning them off about God or threatening them?

What would be **three negative ways**?

IS HE FOR REAL? [the existence of God—Psalm 53]

THIS WEEK

The idea of God's existence has been debated for centuries. Doubters and skeptics are found even among young teens. And then there are those who claim to believe but are actually practicing atheists—they may verbally acknowledge God's existence, but they act as if he isn't alive. This Talksheet is designed to spark thinking and discussion about the existence of God and their way of dealing with those who deny him.

OPENER

Stand by the light switch for this introductory discussion. Ask your students if they have ever seen electricity (none of them have!). Hit the light switch and ask if they are seeing electricity. Point out that they have never seen electricity but only the results of electricity. Ask how many believe in electricity. Ask how many have felt electricity. Use this as a starting point to show its similarity to their faith in God.

Another approach is to use the idea of gravity, again something they've never seen. Pick one of your students to help you illustrate this idea. Have this person lay on the floor with their arms under their back. Hold an egg over their head, and then tell your students that you have come to the conclusion that because you have never seen gravity, there is no such thing. You are now going to "prove" that gravity doesn't exist. Allow your victim to try to talk you out of dropping the egg by arguing that gravity does exist even if you can't see it—it's up to you whether or not you're convinced enough to not drop the egg!

THE DISCUSSION, BY NUMBERS

1. Take some time to talk about these phrases and what the words mean. Make sure that the students know the difference between an atheist (one who believes God doesn't exist) and an agnostic (one who isn't sure).

2. What things most strongly supported God's existence for your kids? Why? What other items would they choose that aren't on this list?

3. Did your kids agree or disagree with these statements? How do they feel about God's existence or his apparent silence? Talk about the ways God is apparent if people care to look—in the lives of others, through his presence in prayer, through his Word, and the like. Allow those with real doubts and questions to have them.

4. Take some time to talk about this description of the human heart. You may want to make a list of their responses on a whiteboard or poster board.

How is human vileness and corruption in evidence today? Have your students discuss examples. Point out the hope that has come to people through Christ's birth, death, and resurrection.

5. What do your kids think are positive—and negative—ways to explain God's existence to others? What is challenging about trying to prove that God is real? How would your kids respond if someone were to challenge their ideas and faith?

THE CLOSE

Summarize the points made about the foolishness of the human heart when it denies God. Point out that those who act as if God doesn't exist are just a guilty as those who profess he doesn't exist. Discuss the fact that there are solid reasons to believe in God, and that faith isn't the same as wishful thinking. Let the students know that it's common to have doubts. But doubts can be resolved by taking time to consider the wonders of God, their experience with him, and the inner voice that tells people he really does exist.

MORE

● You may want to have your kids search the Internet for evidence on the existence of God—or if that's too hard, maybe ask someone in your church or community who can prove the existence of God to speak to your group. Be sure that he or she keeps the material simple enough for your kids to understand. Ask your kids to think of questions to ask and be sure to debrief with your group.

● What other groups—including world religions and cults—are there that deny the existence of the God of the Bible? Some of your kids may have heard about these at school or in class. Wicca, New Age, Theosophy, Buddhism, Eastern cults, Confucianism, and Islam are just a few examples. For more information, check out the Cult Awareness & Information Centre Directory (www.caic.org.au/zentry1.htm) or the World Religions Index (http://wri.leaderu.com).

THE LAST OF THE LOYAL

1. Below are some situations that happen between friends. Which **three** would bother you the most?

   Your friend—
   ❑ Tells everyone your most embarrassing secret
   ❑ Makes a move on your girlfriend or boyfriend
   ❑ Gets into trouble—and blames you
   ❑ Asks you to help cheat at school
   ❑ Cusses you out for no reason
   ❑ Makes the team or club—and you don't
   ❑ Dumps you for a new set of friends
   ❑ Lies to you
   ❑ Steals from your locker
   ❑ Gets involved with drugs, but doesn't tell you
   ❑ Won't admit that he or she borrowed something of yours
   ❑ Gets you in trouble with your mom or dad

2. **Proverbs 18:24** talks about a friend who sticks closer than a brother. What are three qualities that you think make a good friend?

3. Match the following Bible verses with the statements in the right-hand column.

Matthew 5:24	Don't do anything to cause a friend to fall.
Matthew 18:15	Be a devoted friend; hold your friends in high honor.
Matthew 18:21-22	Don't slander or speak against a friend.
Romans 12:10	If a friend wrongs you, talk about it and try to win this friend back.
Romans 14:21	Don't ignore a friend who needs something you can give.
James 4:11	Settle matters quickly when you're at odds with someone.
1 John 3:17	You should be willing to forgive your friends over and over.

4. What is **one thing** that you need to work on in order to be a good friend?

THE LAST OF THE LOYAL [loyalty—Psalm 55]

THIS WEEK

Sooner or later, every teenagers will get hurt by a friend because of shifting loyalties, confused priorities, or selfish interests. This TalkSheet will help your group understand that good friends do their best to remain loyal.

OPENER

Start out by getting your students to talk about physical wounds. Ask the group to describe injuries they have suffered. What's the worst pain they ever experienced? A broken arm or leg? A deep cut? Point out that one of the worst wounds of all isn't really a physical injury, but the pain of a heart broken by the betrayal of a friend. Sometimes emotional scars are worse than physical scars—they just don't show on the outside. Like putting bandages on physical cuts, how can your kids deal with the cuts from a friend's betrayal?

THE DISCUSSION, BY NUMBERS

1. Ask for a few of your kids to share their answers. Then vote to see if your students feel problems such as these are common among young people. You may want to point out that it obviously would be best if these things never happened among friends. Encourage the students to decide in their hearts to be the best friends they can be.

2. According to these verses, what are some qualities of a good friend? Jot ideas on the whiteboard or poster board. Which qualities do your kids think they need to work on? Why? You may want to have them rank themselves on each quality of a friend on a scale of 1-5 (1 being "I really need to work on it" and 5 being "I'm doing good in this area").

3. How did your kids match up these verses? You may want to re-read each verse with the group and talk about how it relates to friendship in their lives today. If you're running short on time, split your group up into smaller groups to read and discuss each passage.

4. What are some areas of friendship that your kids need to work on? Point out that nobody is the perfect, ideal friend. That's one thing about being human. But everyone can work on strengthening friendships and working on being a better friend.

THE CLOSE

Friendship is a gift—to be received and to be given. Ask your kids to think about their friendships. Are they on the taking or the receiving side of all their friendships, or do they give as well? How loyal would your kids rate themselves on a scale of 1 to 10 (1 being "Loyal? What's that?" and 10 being "I'm like glue, man, I'm loyal") ? What can each of your kids do to improve their friendships and their loyalty? And how can God help them to be better friends as well?

MORE

● Girls and guys have different types of friendships. You may want to talk about the differences between friendship among girls and those among guys. What are some differences between them? How do guys relate to each other—and how is this different than how girls relate to each other? Finally, are same-sex friendships the same or different than opposite-sex friendships? Does God expect people to treat boyfriends and girlfriends the same as friends? Why or why not?

● How does the world's view of friendship differ from Psalm 55? You may want to ask your group to think about how the world, society, and the media portray friendship. What do they see on TV or movies? What are good and bad qualities of friendship? And how to these compare to what King David writes about in this proverb? Take some time to talk about these differences and how these affect Christians.

SERVING THE SLUMS

1. Why do you think some people are **homeless**? Check two reasons from the list below.
   - ❏ They're victims of society.
   - ❏ They're lazy.
   - ❏ They're paying the price for not working hard in school.
   - ❏ They're addicts or alcoholics.
   - ❏ They're mentally unstable.
   - ❏ They're unlucky.
   - ❏ They're being punished for doing something wrong.
   - ❏ They made a series of bad choices.
   - ❏ They're victims of unfortunate circumstances.
   - ❏ They're born that way.

2. If you were approached by a stranger who wanted a handout (like money or food), what would you do?

   If you found yourself on the street without food or money, would you beg from people? Why or why not?

3. Check out **Psalm 82**—below are some phrases from verses 2-4. For each phrase, write down one thing that you could do to live out these verses.

   Defend the cause of the weak and fatherless

   Maintain the rights of the poor and oppressed

   Rescue the weak and needy

   Deliver weak and needy from the hand of the wicked

4. When you see a person who is weak, needy, defenseless, or hurting in some way, what do you most often do?
   - ❏ Watch
   - ❏ Say nothing
   - ❏ Walk away
   - ❏ Comfort them
   - ❏ Feel bad
   - ❏ Defend
   - ❏ Pray
   - ❏ Laugh
   - ❏ Say something
   - ❏ Join in
   - ❏ Tell someone
   - ❏ Feel nothing

SERVING THE SLUMS [helping others—Psalm 82]

THIS WEEK

There are so many needy people—poor or homeless people in every suburb, city, and country around the world. Here are people who feel rejected. Here are people crying out for a mom or dad to love them—the oddballs, misfits, and others who don't fit with their peers. This TalkSheet will help your group recognize that they have an obligation to help those whom others would cast away.

OPENER

You may want to have someone unknown to the group impersonate a homeless person. This person should play and dress the part—and be able to address the issues of homelessness and answer difficult questions your kids might have. Some of these may include why they can't get a job or what made them homeless.

For a different twist, you could also ask the manager or someone from a homeless shelter to come in and talk about the problem with the group. Because they have first hand experience, they may be able to share stories about and discuss the problems of a homeless family—food, shelter, medical care, spiritual problems, life-threatening problems, and so on.

THE DISCUSSION, BY NUMBERS

1. Why do your kids think people become homeless? Ask the group to explain the reasons they chose. Give your kids a chance to argue their opinions with each other. What do your kids think is the most common reason that people become homeless?

2. What would your kids do in these situations? What do they think people most often do when someone approaches them for money or food? Why? Ask your group how they would get food and shelter if they found themselves in need.

3. Psalm 82 clearly states the duty of people to help the poor, helpless, and needy. Ask the group to explain their modern examples. How can your kids live out these verses today? You may want to make a list of their ideas on a whiteboard or poster board. Point out that people who are well fed and housed can also be weak, oppressed, or needy (for example, a kid without friends is socially needy). Is this the same as being homeless or hungry? Why or why not? How do your kids think Jesus would respond to both situations?

4. What is the most common reaction that your kids have? Why? Be sure not to make your kids feel guilty for the reactions—most teenagers aren't sure how to react or how to help these people.

THE CLOSE

Teenagers can't save the world, but they can start to think differently about those in need. Point out that homelessness and hurt aren't just problems on the street or in the slums—many kids at their school are crying out for friendship, encouragement, and acceptance. Challenge your group to think about how they can show the love of Christ to others around them. Communicate to your group that it's easy for people to stay comfortable and safe in their own group of friends. What would happen if they stepped out and helped someone outside of their comfort zone?

MORE

● Teenagers sometimes feel threatened when they step out of their comfort zones. Take a look with your group and the life of Jesus. He was the ultimate servant—never in a comfort zone, and always on a mission to help those in need. Check out some stories with your kids about the life of Jesus. You may want to split your group up into smaller groups and have them look for examples of how Jesus reached out to others. There are several stories in Matthew, Mark, Luke, and John. Point out that Jesus didn't worry about fitting in the crowd or having the right friends—he hung out with sinners, lepers, and even a prostitute! He was a true rebel, in the sense that he dared to make a difference in the lives of others—and he was killed for it. How can your kids live like Jesus in their everyday lives? Are they willing to step out and help others in the name of Jesus?

● Try role-playing a homeless situation with your kids—give each of them a specific problem, such as losing their job, getting divorced, being a single parent, suffering from AIDS, being abused at home, hooked on cocaine, being forced into prostitution, and so on. How would they answer those who asked "what is wrong with you"? How would these situations affect their lives? You may want to have other kids question them and see what it's like for the homeless person to explain where they are and why.

GIVING GOD HIS PROPS

1. Which one of these things you would most like to have happen to you?
   - ❑ Someone to write a hit song about me
   - ❑ Someone to form a fan club for me
   - ❑ Someone to write a book about me
   - ❑ Someone to build a Web site about me
   - ❑ Someone to write a feature article about me in a magazine
   - ❑ Someone to design memorabilia about me (like baseball cards or a Barbie doll)
   - ❑ Someone to give me a priceless gift
   - ❑ Someone to build a museum in my honor

2. Check out **Psalm 96**, then fill in the blanks for this paraphrased version.
   Verse 1— _____ to the Lord a new_____.
   Verse 3— _____his glory among the nations.
   Verse 8— Bring an_____ and come into his courts.
   Verse 9— _____the Lord in the in the splendor of his_____.
   Verse 11— Let the heavens_____, let the earth be_____.

3. Could you see yourself doing any of these items? **N (no way)**, **M (maybe)**, or **Y (yup, that's me)**?
   ___ Singing in front of the church or youth group
   ___ Telling others about God
   ___ Defending your beliefs to those at school
   ___ Giving money to the church or charity
   ___ Worshiping God
   ___ Going on a service or missions trip
   ___ Giving thanks to God everyday for his blessings
   ___ Rejoicing because you're a Christian

4. Maybe you can't write a hit song or a book about God, but there are some things you can do. List **four** things you could do for God.

GIVING GOD HIS PROPS [glorifying God—Psalm 96]

THIS WEEK

The greatest confessions of faith throughout the church age all say that the chief purpose of human beings is to glorify God. Psalm 96 gives a list of five ways to do so—sing praise to the Lord, tell others of his glory, give him your best, worship him, and live a life of joyful holiness. Use this TalkSheet to teach your kids the specific things they can do to glorify God.

OPENER

Do your students know how the ancient Canaanites used to glorify their gods? In those days a family that bought or built a new house would dedicate it to the gods. To do so, they would sacrifice one of their children and put the child's remains in an urn in the main room. (You might ask how many in the class wouldn't be around if it was still the custom to sacrifice the firstborn!) How about other world religions or cults? You may want to have your kids check the Internet for information on some other religions.

In contrast, think about God and Jesus. Remind your kids that, thankfully, God doesn't want to be glorified in these ways. He has his own ways to be glorified and honored. Then pass out the TalkSheet to find out how God wants to be celebrated.

THE DISCUSSION, BY NUMBERS

1. Ask your kids to explain what they picked and why. Though some of these things sound wildly improbable, some are actually the sort of things people have done throughout history to worship God. The great hymns of the faith, the books of the Bible, the untold self-sacrifices (and uncountable dollars given by believers!), the shrines, and the "fan club" of the faithful who have tried to imitate Jesus Christ all over the earth—these are all to God's glory.

2. How did your kids fill in these phrases? You may want to go through the verses again and point out that Psalm 96 commands believers to glorify God by singing a new song (verse 1), declaring his glory (verse 3), giving gifts or offerings to him (verse 8), worshiping him, and imitating his holiness (verse 9)—and doing all of this joyfully (verse 11).

3. How did your kids respond to these statements? You may get a variety of responses. Why are some of these things hard for them to do? What keeps them from doing some of them? Point out that glorifying God—like praising a person—isn't easy. It takes effort to give someone else praise.

4. Check out the items that your kids listed. Challenge them to think about doing one of these, either individually or as a group. If you choose to do one as a group, brainstorm how your group can get the ball rolling.

THE CLOSE

Use this opportunity to remind your kids of two important facts about God—first, God is great and worthy to be praised and second, the step toward true worship—that brings real glory to him—is the step of turning one's life over to God. Have your kids turned over their lives to God? Has this changed their life? Take some time to talk about living for God. And if you have some non-Christians in your class, you may want to challenge them to consider receiving Jesus as their Savior—and give them a few minutes in prayer.

MORE

- You may want to plan a worship service for your group next class time (or talk to your minister about a church worship service led by the youth). The service could include posters, reciting of memorized Bible verses, announcements regarding planned fundraisers and fun events, live music (if any), recorded music, prayers, and the like—and, everyone can have a part!

- How do your kids glorify God in their own lives? How often do they do what Psalm 96 says? Take some time to talk about the kinds of music that your kids listen to—or the TV shows or movies they watch. How hard or easy is it to celebrate God in today's society and culture? How are Christians portrayed when they do praise God in public? Discuss some ways that your kids can start to celebrate God in the ins and outs of everyday life.

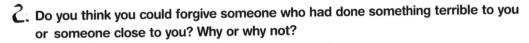

HEAVY-DUTY LOVE

Mr. Smith silently made his way up the frosty steps of the state penitentiary. He unfolded his wool coat for the metal detector and dutifully signed the visitor roster. Mr. Smith seated himself in the paint-chipped chair that faced an empty seat through a thick wall of glass, interrupted by a small, screened speaking hole. Meanwhile, down in the dark halls of the prison, a number was called and a thin man slowly shuffled out of his cell and headed for the visitor area. This convict was spending his life in prison for the brutal rape and murder of a young high school junior, and his visitor—Mr. Smith—was here at the prison on a mission. He was here to tell the killer of his only daughter that he had forgiven him, and that God could forgive him too.

1. Circle your opinion about what Mr. Smith wanted to do.

Crazy	Loving	Strong
Noble	Exemplary	Perverse
Unnecessary	Strange	
Weird	Admirable	

2. Do you think you could forgive someone who had done something terrible to you or someone close to you? Why or why not?

3. Check the description that you think best fits **God's kind of love**.
   - ❑ Loving people who are friends to you
   - ❑ Caring about people who are in trouble but are innocent
   - ❑ Giving people things they want and letting everyone off the hook for wrong actions
   - ❑ Loving people who don't deserve to be loved
   - ❑ Having compassion on people who are rejects but are still likable

4. Check out **Psalm 103**. In your own words, make a list of the things that God's love does for people or provides for people.

5. If you were going to try to imitate God's kind of love, which of the following things would you do?
   - ❑ Stand up for those being put down
   - ❑ Act religious and holy
   - ❑ Give people hugs and act all mushy
   - ❑ Control your temper so that you're slow to get angry
   - ❑ Lecture those who are doing wrong things
   - ❑ Forget about paying back those who have harmed you
   - ❑ Forgive wrongs done toward you
   - ❑ Make people fear you because God is your Father
   - ❑ Other—

HEAVY-DUTY LOVE [Christian love—Psalm 103]

THIS WEEK

Agape love is the highest form of loving expression. This is the kind of love displayed by God—pure, self-giving, unconditional, rare, heavy-duty love. Kids can discover this kind of love and begin to display it in their lives. This TalkSheet introduces this love to your students and encourages them to see how God might show his love through them.

OPENER

What various and insignificant meanings do people have for the word love? You may want to ask your kids to brainstorm all the meanings of love that they know or have learned (or perceived) from society, what they've been taught in school or home, or from friends. What actions does love include? And how is love shown or expressed in culture, on TV, in the movies, in music, in school, at home, or at church? Make a master list of all these meanings, examples, and illustrations. Then talk about which ones fall under the Bible's under definition of love? You may want to check out 1 Corinthians 13 for clear definitions of love and what God thinks of it.

THE DISCUSSION, BY NUMBERS

1. Discuss the case of Mr. Smith and his forgiveness of the person who murdered his daughter. What do your kids think of his actions? Why? Point out the amazing love a person would have to have in order to offer this kind of forgiveness. How do you think Mr. Smith has the ability to forgive this man?

2. Could your kids forgive someone who hurt them or a loved one? Take some time to talk about how easy or hard it would be. Where did your kids rank themselves on the scale? Where would teenagers in general rank themselves? Be sensitive to your group members during this discussion—some of your kids may be dealing with physical or sexual abuse, as well as divorce and more. Why do they think God expects people to forgive people who don't seem to deserve it?

3. God's love—agape love—loves people even when they don't deserve it. Have your kids received agape love from a parent, friend, or teacher? How did it feel to be loved, even when they didn't deserve it? Point out that about Jesus demonstrated this kind of love throughout his lifetime. You may want to read some of the stories of Jesus' life in Matthew, Mark, Luke, or John, and talk about them with the group.

4. Psalm 103 is full of promises for your teenagers. Ask your group to brainstorm modern-day examples of this kind of divine love. Discuss what each one means for your kids, in their lives today—in their schools, homes, and with their friends.

5. How can your kids demonstrate agape love? What other ideas did they come up with? How does agape love compare with simply being nice to someone or doing a favor for them?

THE CLOSE

Summarize the ideas about godly love that have been brought up during the discussion. Point out God wants everyone—every Christian—to show this kind of love for one another. Ask your kids some of these questions—what would society be like if everyone displayed God's kind of love? How would this affect people? Schools? The church? And what keeps people from showing this kind of love? Why?

Point out that by having the Holy Spirit, Christians actually have the power to love people in the same way God does. What attributes of love are your kids missing in their lives? Which ones do they need to work on, based on this psalm and what you've talked about? And how can they begin to show love to others?

MORE

● Ask your students to think of a person they know who needs heavy-duty love, or a person for whom it would take heavy-duty love to treat kindly. Challenge your students to commit themselves to pray every day this week for this person as the first step in acting lovingly. Encourage the group to look for at least one action they can do for this person or one word they can say to this person in the coming week. Then talk about changes, if any, that your kids saw in the other person, in themselves, or in the relationship.

● You may want to spend some time talking about love and mercy—how are the two related? And how did God having mercy on Christians show in the sacrifice of his son, Jesus? Is it harder for your kids to show love to others or to have mercy on them? Why or why not? What does mercy mean to your kids? You may want to explore this concept of mercy elsewhere throughout the Bible, including Exodus 33:19, Deutoromy 13:17, 2 Samuel 24:14, Nehemiah 13:22, Micah 6:8, Matthew 5:7, and throughout the Psalms.

FEAR NOT!

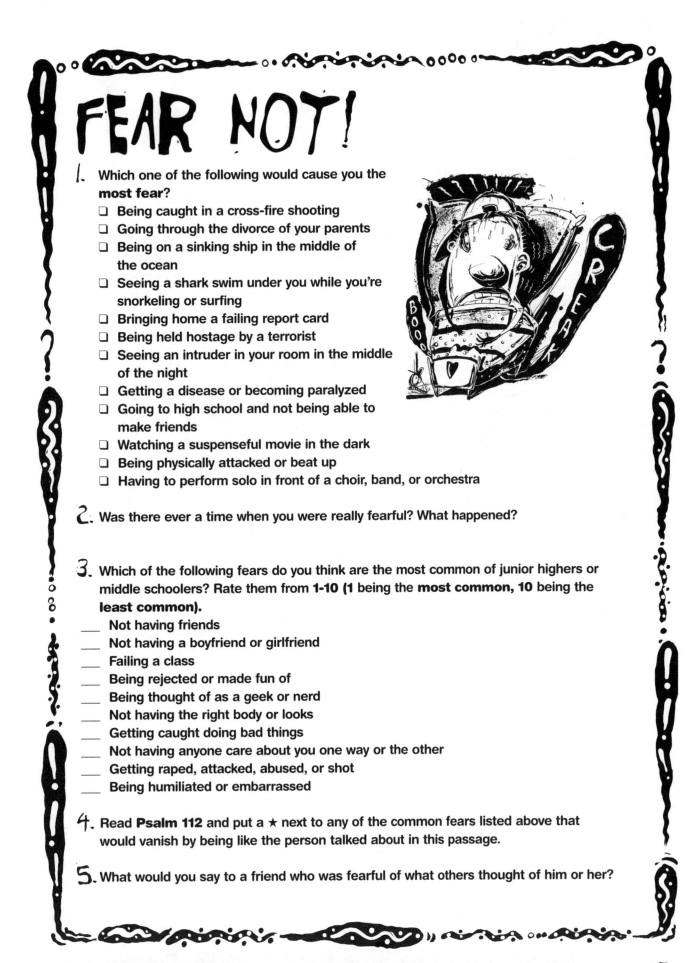

1. Which one of the following would cause you the **most fear?**
   - ❏ Being caught in a cross-fire shooting
   - ❏ Going through the divorce of your parents
   - ❏ Being on a sinking ship in the middle of the ocean
   - ❏ Seeing a shark swim under you while you're snorkeling or surfing
   - ❏ Bringing home a failing report card
   - ❏ Being held hostage by a terrorist
   - ❏ Seeing an intruder in your room in the middle of the night
   - ❏ Getting a disease or becoming paralyzed
   - ❏ Going to high school and not being able to make friends
   - ❏ Watching a suspenseful movie in the dark
   - ❏ Being physically attacked or beat up
   - ❏ Having to perform solo in front of a choir, band, or orchestra

2. Was there ever a time when you were really fearful? What happened?

3. Which of the following fears do you think are the most common of junior highers or middle schoolers? Rate them from **1-10 (1** being the **most common, 10** being the **least common).**
   - ___ Not having friends
   - ___ Not having a boyfriend or girlfriend
   - ___ Failing a class
   - ___ Being rejected or made fun of
   - ___ Being thought of as a geek or nerd
   - ___ Not having the right body or looks
   - ___ Getting caught doing bad things
   - ___ Not having anyone care about you one way or the other
   - ___ Getting raped, attacked, abused, or shot
   - ___ Being humiliated or embarrassed

4. Read **Psalm 112** and put a ★ next to any of the common fears listed above that would vanish by being like the person talked about in this passage.

5. What would you say to a friend who was fearful of what others thought of him or her?

FEAR NOT! [fear — Psalm 112]

THIS WEEK

Sooner or later, fear gets to people. It may not be the terror of things that go bump in the night or a phobia about spiders, but it could very well be the fear of not being accepted or of failing at school. Many junior high or middle school students are often fearful of how they are viewed by their peers. Some are fearful that they will be seen as a coward or a nerd, others that they will be thought of as unattractive or a loser. This psalm offers a great prescription for students or adults who agonize internally about common fears.

OPENER

Divide the room into three parts. Give each section a title such as AIDS, nuclear war, severe acne, unpopularity, or going to hell. Next, ask your students to go to the section of the room that represents what people (in general) fear most. Then ask them to go to the section that represents what people their age might fear most. Finally, ask them to go to the section that represents something that is most likely to happen to at least one of their friends within the next five years. Feel free to use as many titles as you want to use this as a lead-in to talk about personal fears.

Or with your group, make a list of the fears that teenagers today deal with. Write these on a poster board or whiteboard. Now cross out the ones that your kids have control over. Which ones are they able to control (failing grades)? Which ones does only God have control over? And which one are the most common to them and their peers? Why or why not?

THE DISCUSSION, BY NUMBERS

1. What gives your kids the most fear? Ask your kids to explain their fears and which they think is most common among teenagers. Why do some people have different fears than others?

2. Ask for a few volunteers to share their experiences. If you have a large group or are limited on time, break your students into pairs or groups of three and have them share their stories with one another. What was the outcome of the experience?

3. Not everyone has the same fears. Which fears do you think are most common among people their age? Why? Point out that some fears are common, while others are exceptional (like phobias of heights). What do your kids think the difference is between simply being scared and being absolutely terrified?

4. How can fears be relieved by following the advice in the Bible? Would this be easy for your kids to do or not? Talk about how these fears are eliminated by God.

5. Ask the group what advice they'd give based on Psalm 112. What would they say to a friend who wasn't a Christian?

THE CLOSE

God wants your kids to drive fear out of their lives. Challenge them to bring their lives into line with the teaching of the Bible—and to let God give them the peace they want or need. Having those fears doesn't mean that your kids aren't good Christians or cowards—but that they're normal human beings. You may want to close in a time of prayer with your kids and let them spend some time talking with God about their fears.

MORE

- Be sensitive to the fact that you may have kids in your group whose worst fears have come true—maybe they've been in an abusive situation, been a victim of rape or sexual abuse, or been part of a divorce situation. Point out to the group that you are available to talk with—and encourage them to find an adult to help them, if not professional help. For more information and links to helpful sites, visit www.YouthSpecialties.com.

- You may want to have a contest for your students to make a tee shirt design (based on concept rather than quality of art) that expresses the idea that a relationship with God dissolves their fears. Take the winning concept to a person who will turn it into a great artistic design, and have T-shirts made for your group.

PTL

1. When someone says, "**Praise the Lord!**" what do you think they're really saying?
   - ❑ "Rock on, God!"
   - ❑ Nothing, because they don't mean it.
   - ❑ "Amen!"
   - ❑ "Look at me, I'm spiritual!"
   - ❑ "Thanks, God!"
   - ❑ "God gave me my way, again!"
   - ❑ "I can't believe I just got an A on my test!"
   - ❑ Other—

2. What percentage of people do you think really praise God?

3. Check out **Psalm 113** fill in the following blanks with your own words.
   Let the_____of the Lord be praised.
   The Lord is to be praised both_____and_____.
   The Lord is_____over all the nations.
   His glory is_____the heavens.
   He_____the poor and needy from the dust and sits them with_____.
   He makes the childless woman_____ _____.

4. It's one thing to praise God for what he has done, but it's another thing to praise God for who he is and what he is like. Describe in your own words some of the awesome things about God.

5. How would you complete these sentences?

   When I think of what God is like and compare it to what I am like, I feel—

   When I think about what God is like, it makes me want to—

PTL [praising God — Psalm 113]

THIS WEEK

God is worthy of praise. People may thank him from time to time, and they may come to him with their requests and emergencies—but few of them truly praise him for simply being who he is. In praising God for who he is and what he is like, people are forced out of their self-centeredness and into a mode of thinking that quickly humbles them as people measure themselves against the Creator. This TalkSheet will help the group realize that respecting a power far greater than themselves will bring people closer to that power. They will see that praising God isn't just a frivolous expression, but an act of worship.

OPENER

Try the praise circle with your group. With everyone (or small groups) sitting in a circle, ask for a volunteer to go into the middle. The purpose of the game is to praise the person in the middle for something that they've done, something they do, or a positive characteristic that they have. As the adult, be sure to lead this activity and start up the praises if your kids don't. Tell the group that in order to praise this person, it is necessary to be observant and to put a bit of thought into the subject. Let your students know that while it can be fun to praise a friend, it's beneficial, too. People need to hear that they are needed and are important to a group—even those who aren't as actively involved as others. Then point out that God likes to be praised just as much.

THE DISCUSSION, BY NUMBERS

1. Talk about what it really means to praise the Lord—to acknowledge him for who he is and revere him as Lord. Why do some people say it when they don't mean it? How would you feel if someone praised you, but really didn't mean it?

2. Discuss why people don't put much time or effort into giving God praise. What percentage of people do your kids think praise God? What about teenagers in the church? What do your kids think keeps people from praising God?

3. Point out that the writer of Psalm 113 praises God for both who he is as well as what he can and will do for humans. Go through these verses again and come up with a group summary of the verse on a whiteboard or poster board.

4. This will help your students to focus on the attributes of God. Write down the thoughts from the group and then read Psalm 8 and list the attributes on a whiteboard.

5. Discuss the idea that praising God reminds people of their own smallness, of their need for him, and appreciation of him. What kind of behavior changes occur when people realize just how much bigger God is then themselves? How do your kids feel when they stand in the presence of God?

THE CLOSE

You may want to close by reading a poem or lyrics of a song that describe the awesomeness and power of God. If you have a group that likes to sing, pick a song that tells of God's power and awesomeness. Or maybe play a song off a CD that tells of God's greatness. Try to pick a style of music that your kids can relate to, such as a pop song by an artist who is either marketed as Christian or writes Christian lyrics (some mainstream or secular bands write Christian lyrics). Challenge your kids to listen to the lyrics—what is the singer saying about God and why? What is the singer or artist praising God for? You can also find lyrics on the Internet, on the site of nearly every band in the Christian industry. For more information and links, check out CCM Online (www.ccmcom.com), Jubilee Harvest (www.jesusfreak.com/jubilee), The Lighthouse Electronic Magazine (http://tlem.netcentral.net), The Phantom Tollbooth (www.tollbooth.org), or www.YouthSpecialties.com.

MORE

● What makes it hard to praise God? Sometimes it seems like kids don't get any praise from parents, teachers, or friends. So they can't understand how to praise God—someone that they can't see. Take some time to talk about this with your group. What are some ways that they can get closer to God in order to understand his love and power in their lives? You may want to recommend a student Bible or journal for your kids to use. Point out that many things stand in the way of giving God praise, including stress, pain in their lives, and feeling distant from God. How can your kids work though these situations in order to give God the honor he deserves?

● Challenge your students to commit themselves to taking time to praise God every day for a week. Encourage them to keep a journal of what they praised God for each day and maybe have them bring the journals to the next meeting. You may want to have a few volunteers share what they thought and did. How did the activity bring them closer to God? What did your kids learn about what God is doing in their lives?

IDLE IDOLS

1. What **idols** to you think people worship today?

2. Pick the phrase that best describes the idea of worship.
   - ❑ Bowing down in front of an image
   - ❑ Going to some kind of religious service
   - ❑ Singing real loud with your arms up and eyes closed
   - ❑ Dancing around a fire and chanting
   - ❑ Honoring, caring about, obeying, and putting someone or something first
   - ❑ Sacrificing hard-earned money and time
   - ❑ Putting pictures of the object or person you worship all around your room
   - ❑ Lighting candles and incense to channel your thoughts and energy

3. Check out **Psalm 115:2-8**. In your own words, describe the curse in this passage on those who worship false gods.

4. What are some things that junior high or middle schoolers could do to worship God?

5. Do you **agree** or **disagree** with this statement?
   God isn't God unless he is God over all.

   Why or why not?

6. Check out these verses and describe, in your own words, what they mean to you.
   Exodus 20:3-4
   Matthew 6:21
   Matthew 22:37

IDLE IDOLS [putting God first—Psalm 115]

THIS WEEK

Worshiping an idol is the last thing most people think they might be guilty of. It's a primitive act—but it's also a very modern one. Technology hasn't eliminated idols—it has merely replaced them with sleeker, shinier, and more sophisticated models. Kids are surrounded by idols that compete for their worship. Some of the modern idols are made of metal and plastic. Other idols can include the desire to be popular and the ambition to succeed. Idols often have the trademarks of something good. People who are so focused on getting good grades in school that they neglect time with God are in danger of making grades an idol. An idol, in short, is anything that comes before God. Many people are far deeper into worshiping idols than they imagine. Use this TalkSheet to bring these ideas home!

OPENER

Ask your kids if they can define an idol. Help them out if need be (an idol is anything we put in place of God). Then help the students draw or brainstorm a list of some things in their lives—objects, people, goals, or whatever—that can become idols in their lives, and in the lives of others around them. You may want to make a master list of these, or use it to play a Pictionary-type game. What did your kids come up with? What often takes priority in people's lives? Why do people worship these when so many are temporary things? Use these questions and activity to springboard into a discussion on idols.

THE DISCUSSION, BY NUMBERS

1. Discuss whether or not people worship idols today. Using what you talked about in the intro, discuss what some candidates for modern-day idols might be. Are some idols bigger or more important than others? Why or why not?

2. Talk about what it means to worship something or someone. Do any of these statements describe worship accurately? If so, which ones? Finally, ask the group whether a person can worship something that isn't alive.

3. This verse describes people who worship idols as spiritually dead, unfeeling, and blind as the object they worship. Discuss as difference between what happens to idolaters and what happens to those who put God first in their lives.

4. How can your kids worship God in their lives? Most of them don't have a ton of money or know how to worship God. List their suggestions on a whiteboard. Point out that the biggest way to worship God is to put him first in their lives.

5. Do your kids agree or disagree? Ask for a few volunteers share their answers. Reinforce the idea that whatever is first in their life is truly their god.

6. What are these passages saying to your kids—as modern-day teenagers? Ask for some to share their summaries of each verse and discuss how worship is described in the verses. Help your students to develop responses to those passages that are specific to their daily lives.

THE CLOSE

Ask your kids to create a list of things that might become idols in their lives if they're not held in check. Keep a list of these on a poster board or whiteboard. Encourage the group to explain how these idols could become more important than God and why. What may become idols in their lives as time goes by? When they go to high school? To college? When they get married? Talk about these and how they can stay on the right track with God, despite all the potential idols in their lives.

MORE

● How does our materialistic society encourage worshiping idols? What attitudes does society give teenagers about the need for clothes, music, or money? You may want to spend some time talking about society and what influence advertising has on culture and teens. How can your kids avoid getting sucked into the materialistic mentality? Maybe watch some ads with your kids to pick out what is being idolized on TV or in the movies. And how often do they see examples like this throughout the week?

● You may want to create a follow-up questionnaire via mail or e-mail after you've done this TalkSheet. Ask those in your group to do a self-evaluation to see if they have put their actions behind their words as far as making God the number-one priority in their lives. How successful have they been and what has or hasn't helped them? Where would they like God to be in their lives five years from now? Ten years from now?

SOUL POLLUTION

1. The following items can pollute your thinking or negatively affect your relationship with God. List them in order of harmfulness, with **1 being the most harmful**.

___ MTV or VH1
___ Porn magazines
___ TV
___ Radio
___ Newspapers
___ Internet chat rooms
___ R-rated movies
___ Music with vulgar lyrics
___ Magazines
___ Comic books

___ Video games
___ Tabloids
___ *Sports Illustrated* Swimsuit Edition
___ PG-13 movies
___ X-rated movies
___ Internet pornography
___ Gambling
___ Soap operas
___ Talk shows
___ Other—

2. Who do you think should decide what is soul pollution for you? Why?

❑ Parents or guardians
❑ Church leaders
❑ Teachers
❑ Friends
❑ The media

❑ Youth pastor
❑ God only
❑ Society at large
❑ Yourself

3. How do you feel after immersing yourself in **soul pollution**? Circle your choices.

Joyful
Ashamed
Peaceful
Weak

Guilty
Excited
Burdened
Nothing

Fulfilled
Embarrassed
Fulfilled
Other—

4. Check out **Psalm 119:9-16**. What was the question asked?

What was the solution?

SOUL POLLUTION [purity—Psalm 119]

THIS WEEK

Soul pollution is everywhere and kids are soaked in it. TV, movies, friends, music, and more are filling your kids' minds and souls with evil, violence, and sin. The psalm writer saw the same problem in his day. In Psalm 119:9 he asks, "How can a young man keep his way pure?" There is a solution—a set of filters to block the debris of sin—living according to God's Word, seeking God with all the heart, and committing God's Word to memory.

Those who focus on Christ will find themselves losing their taste for the offerings of the world. They will be able to sense the foul odor of soul pollution more quickly. While it's unrealistic to expect that students can avoid all of its influence, they can learn to be selective and careful about what they allow into their minds and hearts.

OPENER

How careful are your kids about what they put into their bodies? Start by asking your group if their parents try to control what they eat and how often. Are they allowed to snack at midnight or to eat ice cream for breakfast? What limits on food and diet have their parents or guardians given them? And why are these limits healthy? What happens if someone doesn't eat right—maybe suffers from an eating disorder or obesity? And what limits are given to junior highers or middle schoolers on drinking? Why is there a legal age limit on alcohol?

The answer is simple—society and their parents are supposed to know what's good for them…that is, in regards to food and alcohol. But some people slip through the cracks and start drinking or smoking underage. Some kids can do whatever they want. And in some cases it shows.

What about restrictions on soul pollution? What restrictions on movies or TV do your kids have? How about music? Point out that just like food, sexual images, violent music, or vulgarity will affect them, whether they know it or not. Take some time to talk about this "feeding" with your kids.

THE DISCUSSION, BY NUMBERS

1. How does soul pollution reach people? Which of these items does your group think has the most potential for damage? Why or why not? You may want to rate these as a group and discuss if any are more harmful than others. And if so, how?

2. Discuss the role of parents, church leaders, teachers, and other adults in giving direction and wisdom in the choices to be made. Why do kids rebel against the rules of their parents? Why do teenagers think that they know best? And what happens when they're wrong?

3. What happens when a Christian is overexposed to soul pollution? Talk about the toxic effect it can have on their relationships with God. You may want to share an example from your own life when you were overexposed to soul pollution or have a few willing students share their examples.

4. Identify the solutions offered in Psalm 119:9-16 to a young person seeking purity—living according to God's Word, seeking God with all their heart, obeying his commands, storing God's Word in their hearts (memorizing Bible verses), and striving to avoid sin. How can your kids incorporate these principles into their everyday lives?

THE CLOSE

The media and its influences won't go away. But your kids do have a responsibility to choose what they watch and read—and keep their heart and soul free from pollution and ungodly influences. Not an easy task to do. Point out that what they put in their minds will affect how they think, interact with, and treat others, themselves, and God. How can your kids develop the wisdom to know what is pollution to their souls? Challenge your kids to set up a set of guidelines for their own lives and how they'll choose what not to see, watch, and listen to.

MORE

● Invite your students to create their own soul pollution rating system for movies, television shows, Web sites, Internet chat rooms, and musical recordings. Tell them to base their evaluations on the aspects of these things that are the most detrimental to their spiritual growth. Maybe list some examples of movies or TV shows and apply these ratings with your group.

● Keep an eye out for your kids who may be caught up in some serious soul pollution—particularly the males in your group. Internet pornography is becoming a common trap for many junior high and middle school boys. You may want to talk about this more with your group and point out the dangers or getting caught up in porn. For more information and links, check out Caught By the Web (www.caughtbytheweb.com), eXXit (www.exxit.org), Focus on the Family's resources (www.pureintimacy.org), or Breaking Free From Pornography (www.porn-free.org).

WASTING TIME

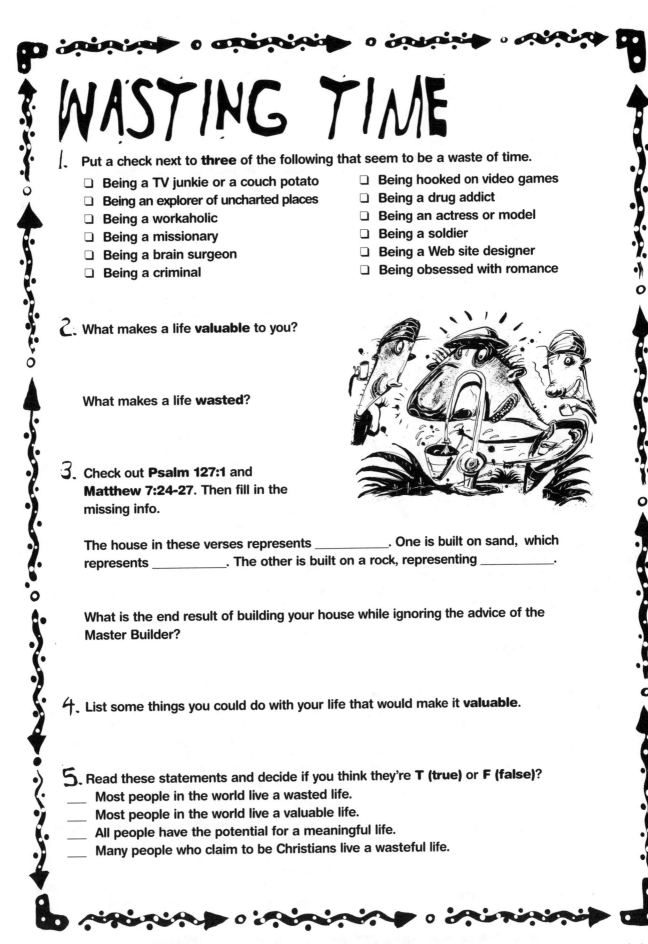

1. Put a check next to **three** of the following that seem to be a waste of time.

   ❏ Being a TV junkie or a couch potato
   ❏ Being an explorer of uncharted places
   ❏ Being a workaholic
   ❏ Being a missionary
   ❏ Being a brain surgeon
   ❏ Being a criminal

   ❏ Being hooked on video games
   ❏ Being a drug addict
   ❏ Being an actress or model
   ❏ Being a soldier
   ❏ Being a Web site designer
   ❏ Being obsessed with romance

2. What makes a life **valuable** to you?

   What makes a life **wasted**?

3. Check out **Psalm 127:1** and **Matthew 7:24-27**. Then fill in the missing info.

   The house in these verses represents _____. One is built on sand, which represents _____. The other is built on a rock, representing _____.

   What is the end result of building your house while ignoring the advice of the Master Builder?

4. List some things you could do with your life that would make it **valuable**.

5. Read these statements and decide if you think they're **T (true)** or **F (false)**?
   ___ Most people in the world live a wasted life.
   ___ Most people in the world live a valuable life.
   ___ All people have the potential for a meaningful life.
   ___ Many people who claim to be Christians live a wasteful life.

WASTING TIME [your purpose in life—Psalm 127]

THIS WEEK

The students in your group have most of their lives in front of them. They can still reach the goals and dreams they aspire to—they can invest in things that will enrich their lives in the future and pay off in the present. But life can wasted, too. Not every investment pays off positively. The only way to invest a life so that it has meaning and purpose is to place it in God's hands. This TalkSheet will underscore the need to wisely construct their lives according to the will of God in order to live a life that isn't squandered on crumbling things.

OPENER

Start by writing this statement on a whiteboard or poster board—THE GREATEST SIN A PERSON CAN COMMIT IS THAT OF A WASTED LIFE. Ask your kids how they feel about this statement and whether they agree or not. What do they think about the following situations?

- A talented writer drops out of college and ends up doing factory work to support his family.
- A woman decides not to have kids in order to focus on her career.
- A bum lives on the street, with no money or home, but loves the Lord.
- A musician produces a few hits, but then succumbs to drug abuse and alcohol.
- A student decides to quit high school and spend his days surfing and hanging out.
- A politician is a good person, but isn't a good leader for his country.

Spend some time discussing these and other situations. Point out that although it isn't your place to judge the lives of these people, it's hard to tell what is a wasted life. Ask for your kids' input and how they view spending life and living for God.

THE DISCUSSION, BY NUMBERS

1. Which activities do your kids think are a waste of time? Which do they think are profitable ways to live? Invite them to add other things to this list. Let them debate their ideas among themselves.

2. Your kids may have different opinions on how to make life valuable—or waste it. Discuss what it takes to make a life valuable and what wastes a life. You may want to make a list of your group's thoughts.

3. How did your kids fill in these verses? You may want to read the verses again and point out again that the house stands for their lives, the rock represents the foundation of the teachings of Christ, and the sand stands for the lack of

foundation in those who ignore Christ's words. Remind them that a life lived outside of God's plan can lead to a wet and slippery end.

4. Have the group share specific things that they could do to give their lives eternal value and meaning. Help them think of tangible ways to do this, such as telling a friend about Christ, building strong friendships, showing love toward a person others ignore, and so on.

5. Discuss the fact that most people are living lives empty of eternal meaning and purpose—a vain life, as the psalmist puts it—because they don't allow God to be the one who calls the shots in their lives. Point out that this is true for many Christians as well. Challenge your students to invest their time and energy into following God's way for their lives.

THE CLOSE

Close by pointing out that it's important to have goals for life—even short-term goals. God often shapes and leads people in their goal-setting. Have your kids write down three goals for things they'd like to do in the next three years. How about the next 10 years? What are three things that they'd like to do before they die? Now ask your group if these goals will affect others as well as themselves? Do any of these goals including reaching out to others or sharing Christ's love? Challenge your kids to keep God in their goal setting and look for ways to honor him in their lives.

MORE

- Do you know any people in your community or church who are Christians and are leading lives rich in meaning and in the guidance of God? You may want to encourage your students to write these people short letters asking them about their life, how they've been able to stay on track with God's plan, and what advice they have to help the young writers plot an equally worthwhile course. Or maybe invite one of these people in to talk with your group about living lives that are worthy to God and to others.

- You may want to read or study some Bible stories or verses about people who lived worthy lives and who had a great impact on others for the Lord. A few examples include Esther, Moses, Paul, and many more. Maybe read a story or two and ask them if these characters thought that they were living a worthy life. Did Moses seem confident? Did Paul seem like the ideal Christian? How about Esther? Point out that many of these characters did think they were worthy to serve God. But God used them in extraordinary ways. Just think about how God can use you and your kids.

HE KNOWS YOU

1. How well do you think God knows you when you're first created (not even born)?

◆ ▮▮▮▮▮▮▮▮▮▮▮▮▮▮▮▮▮▮ ◆

He knows me inside out   He has no idea who I am.

2. Check out Psalm 139:13-16 and decide if each statement is **T (true)** or **F (false)**.

___ God himself knits life in the womb.

___ God doesn't make each one of people individually—it's purely accidental.

___ God creates babies who are born with defects.

___ God observes, but doesn't necessarily tamper with the development of a person.

___ God's handiwork and creation is destroyed by an abortion.

___ God didn't create those who have disabilities.

___ God designs the amount of time for a person to live.

___ God is in control of conception—no baby is an accident.

___ God sometimes makes ugly or unattractive people.

___ God gives each of people the amazing gift of life.

3. What do you think?

People who are unhappy about how they look—

❏ are telling God that he did a bad job

❏ are selfish and vain

❏ are too sensitive

❏ are too hard on themselves

❏ aren't content with the blessings they have

❏ aren't appreciative of all they have

❏ are always going to be unhappy with how they look

❏ are stuck unless they can afford a good plastic surgeon

4. How do you feel, knowing that God is involved in your creation?

Rank these in the order of importance (1 being the most important).

___ I should appreciate how I look.

___ I should respect and obey God's rules for my life

___ I should protect the lives of the unborn.

___ I should see the physically impaired as part of God's design.

___ I should be in awe of the creation process.

___ I should feel extremely special and loved by God.

___ I should aware that God has a plan for my life.

___ Other—

HE KNOWS YOU [the sanctity of life—Psalm 139]

THIS WEEK

Kids have heard the phrase, "All [people] are created equal" but most of them don't believe that it's true. All they have to do is look around them and see that some people are far less equal than others. Some people are extremely beautiful or handsome, and some aren't. There are those who are mentally or physically gifted, and those who operate under a handicap.

This TalkSheet explores the truth that God has his hand on their lives from the moment of conception. He brings, develops, and sustains life—and allows the assembly of genes that give one person a large nose and another acne. God is involved in the creation process of every human being. His direct acts of creation make the idea of abortion a reprehensible problem for most Christians. His plan for each life starts at conception and his plan is good.

OPENER

On a whiteboard write the words PHYSICAL SKILL, MENTAL ABILITIES, and GIFT/TALENT. Ask those in your group to describe anyone they know who excels in any one of these three areas. For example, who do they know that is a child prodigy? Have they seen someone their age who can play the piano like Mozart (who was writing symphonies at age seven!)? How about those who excel at athletics, vocal music, academics, or some other area? Take some time to brainstorm with your group and make a list of all these skills and traits that some have been given. Ask your students to come up with some ideas as to why these people can do what they can do.

Point out that this session will explore the idea that God—from the very start—designs not only these people with exceptional skills, but average and physically or mentally challenged people as well. So no matter what their skill or ability, God's created them all for a purpose!

THE DISCUSSION, BY NUMBERS

1. How well do your kids think God knows them? Take a poll of your group members to see what they think. Then put a check at the very end of the scale (on the side that says "He knows me inside out"). Are they surprised to know that God knows them this well—even before they're born?

2. After reading Psalm 139, make a list of the ideas that are found there. Did your group agree or disagree with these statements? Help the students to apply these truths to their own creation and the creation of others who have different abilities than they do.

3. What message do people give God when they feel unattractive? Discuss how people should think and feel about their own looks. It's true that not everyone can look perfect all the time, give examples of people who are attractive for other reasons besides their looks (personality, sense of humor, and so on), and people who are unattractive, even though they're beautiful on the outside (greed, selfishness, wickedness, and so on).

4. What impact does this psalm have on your kids? How did they order these statements? You may want to go through each one with the group and talk about the importance of each one. Encourage your group to appreciate how God has made them.

THE CLOSE

As you close, encourage your kids to thank God for the unique traits or talents that he's given them. At the same time, be aware of the insecurities and low self-esteems that your kids may have. Low self-esteem is a result of feeling unattractive or unappreciated. You may want to talk about insecurities and self-esteem with the group. When do they feel insecure or unattractive? Why? Who makes them feel insecure?

Point out that everyone feels insecure (it's human) and that God loves people unconditionally. You may want to close in prayer with your kids and remind them that above all—no matter what society or the media says about looks and abilities—God loves them all the same.

MORE

● In light of today's pressure on teenagers, you may want to talk with your kids about God's views of self-esteem and self-image. The majority of teenagers struggle with how they feel about themselves—and some succumb to eating disorders, drug abuse, depression, suicide, and more. For more information on eating disorders and more, check out the American Anorexia Bulimia Association, Inc. (www.aabainc.org), About.com (http://eatingdisorders.about.com), Center for Disease Control and Prevention (www.cdc.gov), or www.YouthSpecialties.com for additional links and info.

● You may want to have someone you know come in and talk about how they've learned to cope with the challenges they face—maybe a handicap or other disability that they've dealt with. How has God worked in their lives to make them stronger Christians and have a closer relationship with God? How did they deal with feeling insecure and inadequate? And how have their challenges affected how they think about themselves and others?

DIVINE DESERT

1. Have you ever felt that God was **distant** from you and that spiritual things were **uninteresting**? On a scale below, where would you rate your feelings about God and spirituality right now?

spiritual stuff is a complete bore   I'm the closest to God I've ever been

2. Check the statement that you think is the most accurate.
   A Christian who feels spiritually dry inside—
   ❑ is caught up in some serious sin
   ❑ isn't growing by reading the Bible, praying, or going to church
   ❑ is just imagining everything
   ❑ shouldn't worry—it's not his or her fault
   ❑ is working too hard to do good
   ❑ is a solid, committed Christian who is having a spiritual low

3. Check out **Psalm 143:4-10** and write in your own words how the author of this psalm is feeling.

4. What do you think a person should do when they feel spiritually dry? Give a grade to each response, just like the grading system at school (A, B, C, D, or F).
   ___ Give up being a Christian.
   ___ Stop going to church or reading the Bible until she feels different.
   ___ Don't say anything to anyone or people might think he's a failure as a Christian.
   ___ Ask for prayer.
   ___ Tell God about it.
   ___ Tell an older or more mature Christian about how she feels.
   ___ Get over it and get on with life.
   ___ Become depressed.

5. Which statement do you think should determine a person's Christianity?
   ❑ How close to God or how spiritual people feel at any given moment
   ❑ The fact that they're really a child of God and that he wouldn't abandon people

DIVINE DESERT [spiritual dry spells—Psalm 143]

THIS WEEK

Every Christian goes through ups and downs in their faith. Junior high and middle schoolers are no exception, but many of them haven't had the experience in the Christian life to know what is going on inside. They often panic or take the flatness as a signal that it's time to look elsewhere for spiritual fulfillment. There aren't always simple reasons for spiritual dryness. Kids will often think that it's the result of some sin in their life. While this can be the case, dry periods often show up in the lives of those who are living exemplary Christian lives. This TalkSheet is designed to help young people understand that spiritual dryness happens to the best among people and that the Christian life isn't driven by feelings.

OPENER

Ask the group who has a relative living the furthest away geographically. Next, find out who has a relative that they haven't heard from in over a year. For those who have family far away, how do they keep in touch? How often to they e-mail or talk on the phone? Do they write letters? What's the longest they've gone without seeing or talking with that person? Use these questions to talk about what it takes to maintain a long-distance relationship. It's hard work. Use some of these ideas to introduce the first discussion question.

THE DISCUSSION, BY NUMBERS

1. How did your kids rank themselves? You may not want to ask for specific answers. Instead, take a poll to see how many of them are more toward the right side of the scale. How about the right side? Point out that everybody isn't at the same point spiritually.

2. Talk about the fact that spiritual ups and downs have many different causes—and that not all of them are related to something people have or haven't done. Even the greatest Christians feel distant from God at times. This doesn't mean that God has distanced himself from them—-but people have distanced themselves from God.

3. How do your kids think the author was feeling while writing this psalm? Make a list of their responses. Have any of your kids felt the same way sometime? Point out that the psalmist didn't identify any particular reason for feeling so distant from God—sometimes there is no specific reason.

4. What are some positive ways to respond to spiritual lows? Which of these answers seem to be the best? The worst? What can your kids tangibly do to help their spiritual lives? What are some ways that they can get back on track with God?

5. Explore the idea that the fact of their relationship with God is what determines the reality of their faith, not their emotional state at a given time. The human emotions are so shaky. But God is constant—the same all the time. Humans fail and fall short, but God never does.

THE CLOSE

Sum up what your group has discovered about spiritual ups and downs—its causes and the relationship between faith and feelings. Point out that everyone—yourself and your kids included—will have ups and downs in their strength of faith. Encourage them to notice when they're feeling dried out and when they need to get closer to God. Remind them that God loves them all the time, even through the down times. You may want to read Psalm 143 again, aloud with your group.

MORE

● Are your students assured of God's presence? You may want to have your students go on a search through the Bible for verses that assure them of God's presence at all times. You may want to have a Bible concordance or index ready for them to use. Read some of these verses with your group and maybe make a list of verses for your kids to hang on to for reference later.

● Or have your kids make a chart or graph of their spiritual patterns. When do they feel the most down or dry in their faith? What experiences bring them closer to God and back on track? Encourage them to pay attention to the patterns they see and how they can avoid this in the future. For example, they may feel distant when they don't read the Bible or pray for days in a row. Or if they spend too much time listening to violent or vulgar music, or watching TV or movies. What role does society and the media play in their spiritual dryness?

SMART LIVING

1. Where or who would you go to if you wanted to get **help** for a problem?
   - ❏ A music legend
   - ❏ A college professor
   - ❏ An advice columnist
   - ❏ A book called *Smart Answers for Dummies*
   - ❏ A football star
   - ❏ A bag lady
   - ❏ A minister or youth pastor
   - ❏ A friend your own age
   - ❏ An older brother or sister
   - ❏ A teacher
   - ❏ A psychic hotline
   - ❏ An Internet chat room
   - ❏ A parent or adult relative
   - ❏ A complete stranger
   - ❏ A telephone hotline operator
   - ❏ A person with a college degree
   - ❏ A police officer
   - ❏ Other—

2. From the list above, put an arrow by those that you **respect** and **trust**.

3. Suppose you were about to be ushered into the presence of God himself. Circle **three** words that might describe your feelings.

Curious	Terrified	Self-assured
Relaxed	Happy	Fearful
Upset	Concerned	Awestruck
Embarrassed	Respectful	Nervous
Joyful	Reckless	
Cautious	Unconcerned	

4. Read **Proverbs 1:7** and then write in your own words what you think this verse means.

5. What do you think your behavior should be like if you take this passage seriously?

6. Put an X on the line to show the degree of **fearful respect** you think you have toward God.

   ◆ |||||||||||||||||||||| ◆

   None at all   All of my awe

SMART LIVING [respecting God—Proverbs 1]

THIS WEEK

This TalkSheet is designed to help students consider the relationship between a respectful fear of God and the ability to make wise choices. Since teenagers often seek wisdom from many not-so-good, unwise sources, it's vital to establish the rationale and source for godly wisdom. By the end of this session, students will be able to determine their own degree of respect for God.

OPENER

Start off this discussion by asking your students if they've ever received an electrical shock. What was the experience like? Did they stick their fingers in a socket? Rub their socked feet on the carpet and then touch someone else? How did they get the shock? Were they surprised at the power of a regular house current? And most importantly, what did they learn in relationship to electricity?

From the day they're born, kids are taught to respect the power of electricity—not to touch downed wires, to be careful around appliances and water, and to keep children away from power outlets. And you still can't see electricity, even if you try.

God's awesome power is parallel—people should fear and respect his person and the wisdom that comes from this reverential fear.

THE DISCUSSION, BY NUMBERS

1. Who do your kids most value and respect for their wisdom? Make a list of their top choices and ask them to explain who or what they chose and why. Did your group list any other sources?

2. See how many of your kids arrowed the items from the list that they checked. If so, why did your kids pick these people for both wisdom and respect? Point out that wisdom and respect go hand in hand.

3. How would your kids feel in the presence of God? Get a feel for the group's feeling as a whole. Point out that a healthy view of God is one that mixes awe, reverence, and respectful fear (such as how one would approach electricity after a good shock). Many people today have lost the sense of God's tremendous majesty and incredible power. People rarely seek wisdom from individuals they don't respect.

4. Ask for a few willing volunteers to share their paraphrases and comments. You may want to write these on a whiteboard and come up with a group paraphrase of the verse.

5. How will your kids apply this verse to their lives? Ask for specific examples of behaviors at home, school, church, and elsewhere. You may want to make a list of these on a poster board or whiteboard.

6. Where do your kids land when it comes to real respect and reverence towards God? If you don't want to ask for specific responses, ask the group (as a whole) how many of them are more toward the right or left of the scale. Where would your kids like to rank themselves in a year? Five years? 10 years?

THE CLOSE

God motivates people to serve him by his incredible power, but he can't and won't force people to respect and have awe for him. Respecting God is a choice, just like choosing to love and serve him. And when he shows people his unconditional love and power, people stand in awe of him more and more. Point out that those who truly fear God have a genuine desire to be obedient to his will. The path to foolish and destructive living is to deny God the respect and position in their lives that he deserves. Where are your kids with their relationships to the one awesome God?

MORE

● Brainstorm with your kids or have your students think of other examples of things they respectfully fear. A few examples include the power of nature—especially the high winds or forceful waves. What other ones are there? Tell them to consider how those things that they respectfully fear compare to God Almighty. Challenge them to reevaluate what they respect and don't respect in light of God's priorities.

● Some teenagers think that they can be fearless—that no one can stand in their way. You may want to talk with your group about fearlessness. What are the dangers of being fearless? What consequences occur then someone does not respect authority, nature, or others? Point out that fearlessness is naive—it is unwise and foolish because no person has the power that God has. What kids or adults do your kids know that portray fearless attributes? And is the degree of their fearlessness healthy or not?

CORRUPTION ABDUCTION

1. If your friends wanted to get you to do something that you knew wasn't right, what kind of bait (food, money, stuff, people, and so on) could they use to snag you?

2. What percentage of students your age do you think would probably do what all the rest of their friends were doing (insert an X on that spot)?

100%   75%   50%   25%   0%

3. Check out **Proverbs 1:10-19**. How might a foolish kid respond to those words? What about a wise kid? Write your answers below.

   Foolish kid—

   Wise kid—

4. This proverb says that the people who do wrong get trapped in their own net. How can people get trapped in the nets of their own creation?

5. What do you think? Do you **A (agree)** or **D (disagree)** with each of these statements?
   ___ Someone with friends who do wrong things should change friends.
   ___ Someone with friends who do wrong things should try to change their behaviors.
   ___ Someone with friends who do wrong things is likely to do those things too.

From *Junior High-Middle School TalkSheets Psalms and Proverbs—Updated!* by Rick Bundschuh and Tom Finley. Permission to reproduce this page granted only for use in the buyer's own youth group. www.YouthSpecialties.com

63

CORRUPTION ABDUCTION [unhealthy friendships—Proverbs 1]

THIS WEEK

Many young teens assume that they are their own person and are influenced little by their friends. Those who observe teens for any length of time have just the opposite opinion. This TalkSheet is designed to help students see that the enticement of bad friends can lead them down paths toward unhappiness and regret.

OPENER

Use your noodle. Start by putting a few dollar bills in the bait slots of several mousetraps. Then set the traps and divide your group into teams. Give each team a few uncooked spaghetti or pasta noodles. With the noodles, each team must retrieve the dollar—but without springing the traps. Use this activity as a way to introduce the first discussion question.

Or brainstorm with your group about the different types of traps and baits—mousetraps, fishing lures, salt licks, and the like. Those that hunt or fish in your group will know a few of these. Talk about how each of them works, what kind of creature it works with, what kind of bait is used, and how likely it is that the creature will escape from the trap. How do these lures and traps compare with those (figurative) traps that people use on each other?

THE DISCUSSION, BY NUMBERS

1. What would your kids most likely be tempted with? Make a list of their suggestions and ideas. Do your kids think others are aware of their weak spots? Why or why not? In what different cases would your kids be tempted by different things, such as food, money, cigarettes, or drugs?

2. What percentage did your group come up with as a whole? Some of them may have varying opinions and the reasons for the variance. Let them defend their opinions with the group.

3. Ask the group to list their answers and make a master list on a whiteboard or poster board. Then ask how many of your kids have heard the same responses coming from their friends. Point out the relevance of these verses to the lives of teens today.

4. What do your kids think? Do they know people who've tangled themselves up with their own poor choices? What would these people have been thinking as they made the choices that snared them?

5. Do your kids agree or disagree? Point out how people can use wisdom to evaluate the influence of friends. Talk about how easy or difficult it is to break of from friends who aren't good influences. What opportunities or dangers are involved in trying to influence those friends for good?

THE CLOSE

Although many of people think they are the exception, the truth is that bad company really does corrupt good morals. People must be very careful about who they choose to hang out with, because not all will have their best interests in mind. God may use people to influence their friends towards good. In fact one of the greatest things a young teen can do is to draw friends toward God, but people must be strong in the faith and realize their own limitations and areas of weakness. That's the balance of giving without giving too much. Spend some time talking about this with your kids. What do they think? How strong are they when dealing with friends, peers, and family members?

MORE

● People reach out to others in different ways. Some people are pastors, some teachers, and some singers. Being a witness of others for Christ is unique to each person. Challenge your kids to think of one way that they can reach out to those around them throughout the week and beyond. Dare them to go out of their comfort zones and to see what happens when God uses them in their everyday lives!

● Point out to your kids that getting snagged in the wrong crowd can be a gradual process—but it's one they'll face in high school, college, and beyond. You may have kids in your group who are in these situations already, hanging with the tough kids, smoking, or doing drugs. Be careful not to come off as judgmental. Instead encourage your kids to think about what they're doing and what others around them are doing. Are they fitting in or standing out? Take some time to talk about the struggles that your kids may be facing and the powerful influence of peer pressure.

CORE FOR LIVING

1. How can you tell when someone is **smart**? Rank the criteria below in order of importance for showing smarts, with 1 being the smartest quality.

___ How well they do in school
___ How quickly they learn a skill
___ How they use their intelligence
___ How good they are at sports
___ How few mistakes they make
___ How respected they are by others

___ How well they get along with others
___ Who they hang out with
___ How well they do their particular job
___ How high their IQ test scores are
___ Who they date
___ Other—

2. What if you were to take a newly developed intelligence test? One hundred points equals a genius and zero points makes you a total dud—how do you think you rate?

   How many points do you think you'll have by age 30?

3. Have you ever thought you were totally right about something, then it turned out you were wrong?

   What happened and how did you feel?

4. Check out **Proverbs 3:5-6** and write down the three most important ideas stated in these verses.

5. If you can't trust your own heart and thoughts, **who** or **what** can you trust?

❑ Your friends
❑ Internet resources
❑ Your pastor
❑ Books or magazines

❑ Media celebrities
❑ Yourself
❑ Your teachers
❑ Your Bible

❑ Your coach
❑ No one
❑ Your government
❑ Other—

6. How can someone like you **acknowledge** God in all of your ways?

CORE FOR LIVING [trusting God—Proverbs 3]

THIS WEEK

Young teens are in the process of making the break from the adults in their lives and becoming their own individuals. Part of this process is moving away from trusting their parents' word to thinking on their own. They most often start to turn toward groups of friends, the tug of awakening senses, or the usually immature logic of their own thinking. This TalkSheet will help students to learn that God wants teens and adults alike to abandon all pretenses of wisdom and seek his ways.

OPENER

Create a thinking cap out of an old hat, some weird decorations, and glue. Get a hold of some fun prizes, a timer, and some trivia questions for a game of Brain Head. Have your group sit in chairs around the room, and set your timer for five minutes. When you read a question, the first person to stand may answer. If the answer is correct, this person gets to wear the thinking cap. Ask another question and if someone else answers correctly, that person gets the thinking cap. Keep this up until the timer rings, then award a prize to whoever is wearing the hat at the time. If time allows, reset the timer and start again. Use this game as an introduction to the topic of how to be a smart thinker.

THE DISCUSSION, BY NUMBERS

1. Explore what qualities define smartness to your students. Rank these again as a group and note the top five that the group suggests. Which one does your group consider to be most important? Why or why not?

2. How would your kids rate themselves? You may not want to ask for specific responses—instead, ask how the average teenagers would rate themselves? How smart would your kids like to be by the time they're 30 years old? Does intellegence change with age—or do people simply learn more?

3. Ask for a few volunteers to share their experiences and possibly add an experience of your own. Point out that all of people—no matter how brilliant they think they are—can be absolutely wrong at the very time they and others think they're right.

4. Make sure the students have identified the three ideas (trust in God with all your heart, don't rely on your own understanding, and acknowledge God in all that you do). Note that the Bible teaches that human thinking—and all the intelligence in the world—can't be trusted. God alone is the only one who has the wisdom to guide their lives. What could happen to someone who tried to figure out life on their own?

5. Who do your kids trust for wisdom and guidance? Talk about where and how to get God's wisdom and guidance—through his Word, prayer, and the counsel of those around people (family, trusted Christian ministers, and caring friends).

6. Discuss what it means to acknowledge God in all areas of life. What are some specific ways that your kids can do this? Talk about how what people say and do sends a message to others about God.

THE CLOSE

Not even the greatest amount of human genius or understanding is safe enough to use as a map for getting through this world. Point out that God's ideas, values, and directions are what it takes to walk a straight road. His words are found in the Bible and through prayer.

Tell the kids that King Solomon was one of the wisest people in the Bible. And he understood that a person who is truly smart will realize that God is smarter still, and will try to discover what he has to say about the various choices facing people in life. A truly wise person will follow what God says, even if it doesn't seem to make sense at the time.

MORE

● You may want to collect videotaped interviews from people who have learned the hard way that God's way of thinking makes more sense than leaning on their own understanding. Show the interviews to your students and talk about the individual examples. What is good or bad about learning the hard way? Why does God sometimes let people mess up before they get things right? Remind them that God is all about second chances—it's never to late to get right with him and follow his wise guidance!

● How do the verses from this proverb compare to what society thinks is wise? What does the media—TV, movies, music, Internet—say about being wise and smart? What stereotypes of smart or wise people has society created? Are these fair and accurate? Take some time to talk about the media's perception of wisdom and how this affects society and your kids—and their peers.

RANDOM ACTS OF GOODNESS

1. What if some of your friends saw someone being mugged or attacked on the sidewalk outside your house? Put a **B** by the **best** thing you could do and a **W** by the **worst**.

___ Get a video camera and tape the attack.
___ Get Dad's shotgun.
___ Run outside and scream and yell.
___ Call 911 and watch what happens.
___ Close the window blinds and watch TV.

___ Run for the first aid kit.
___ Call the neighbors.
___ Command your dog to attack the mugger.
___ Follow the attacker at a distance.
___ Try and mug the mugger or attacker.

2. Read **Proverbs 3:27-28**. What does this verse say is the responsibility of a Christian?

3. If you knew someone was hungry and cold, when would it become your responsibility to do something about it?

___ When they're on my doorstep
___ When they're on my street
___ When they're near death
___ When they're in my city
___ When they're in my state
___ When they're in my country

___ When they ask me to help
___ When I know about it
___ When I become an adult
___ When I have plenty of money
___ When it is my family
___ When it is me

4. The following is a list of things that everyone has the power to do. What are some practical ways you could do each of these things?

Say a kind word—
Express gratitude—
Listen—
Help—

Share—
Encourage—
Give—
Care—

5. How would the world be different if people realized that they're accountable for the actions of other people—both for what they do and what they don't do?

RANDOM ACTS OF GOODNESS [good deeds—Proverbs 3]

THIS WEEK

Christian young people often are bombarded with actions or activities that are to be avoided. They are encouraged less frequently to engage in actions and activities that do good to those they have the power to help. It is these acts that spell out the reality of faith to others. This TalkSheet encourages your young people to explore options that can stretch their faith in practical ways.

OPENER

What if each of your kids could be president for one day—with the power to do all kinds of things? Have your students share what they would do if they had that kind of power at their fingertips. Some may suggest ideas that are self-serving or unrealistic—others may come up with ideas that are very positive. Make a master list of their suggestions on a poster board or whiteboard. Point out that all of them would use the power available to them for something.

THE DISCUSSION, BY NUMBERS

1. Which of these behaviors would the best thing to do? How about the worst? Let them defend their opinions and decide as a group what would be the best solution and why.

2. Ask for some volunteers to share their answers. You may want to go back and read this verse as a group. Point out that Christians are responsible to do good when they have the opportunity.

3. At what point would your kids get involved and why? How could your kids help someone who was hungry and cold in third-world country on the other side of the world? What are some specific ways that your kids could get involved?

4. How would your kids put these things into action in their own lives? How could these powers bring good to a situation? Talk about their responses and make a list on a poster board or whiteboard. Do your kids feel that they really can't do good—because of their age or lack of experience? Why or why not?

5. How does accountability change a person's responsibility? Does accountability change the way your kids think about the power to do good and make a differernce? Why or why not?

THE CLOSE

Challenge the students to consider putting their faith into action in small but powerful ways. While people may not have people starving for food near people, people often know people who are starving for acceptance and kindness. People can express thanks and gratitude to parents, teachers, and friends. Everyone can find opportunities to serve in simple ways. What practical things can your kids do right now?

MORE

● You may want to plan a reach-out or service event with your group—maybe by cleaning part of the church, preparing and delivering a meal for a shut-in, or another project. Or look into something more long term, like supporting a child overseas or becoming a missionary partner. For more information, check out Compassion International (www.ci.org), World Vision (www.wvi.org), or www.YouthSpecialties.com for more links and service-related information and resources.

● Split your group up into small groups and have them check out the Bible for more verses on helping others and showing God's love. If God clearly shows that doing good is a good thing, why have people and society given do-gooders a bad image? Why has doing good become a negative thing among some people? Point out that those who love God want to do good—out of love and gratitude to God. What attitudes are your kids mirroring to each other and to others around them?

SLACKER'S ANONYMOUS

1. How would you define **laziness**?

2. Match the **acts of laziness** (on the left) with their **consequences** (on the right).

___ Late to work—
___ Watch too much TV—
___ Don't bother to shower for a few days—
___ Skip team practice—
___ Don't get around to doing homework—
___ Plagiarize off the Internet—
___ Decide not to do devotions—
___ Don't bother to practice musical instrument—
___ Sleep in too late—
___ Put off cleaning your room—

a. Fail the class.
b. Make a strange noise at the band concert.
c. Fail the assignment and face the law.
d. Start to smell and gross everyone out.
e. Miss out on most of the day.
f. Become distant from God.
g. Make the coach mad and lose your starting position.
h. Rush to get the chores done at the last minute.
i. Get a brain full of mush.
j. Get fired.

3. Check out **Proverbs 6:6-11**. What does this passage say will happen to the lazy person?

   What example is given of the industrious person?

   What qualities does the ant display?

4. Would you bail the lazy man out of his troubles?

   Why or why not?

5. Which statement is most true for you?
   ❑ I feel much better about myself and my life when I've been productive and worked hard.
   ❑ I feel much better about myself and my life when I lay around and do nothing.

6. What areas of life do you tend to be lazy in?

SLACKERS ANONYMOUS [laziness—Proverbs 6]

THIS WEEK

Everyone has 24 hours in a day, yet some people seem to get a whole lot done with those hours while others barely get off the couch. One of the biblical principles to security and godliness is that of wise productivity. Young people are beginning the practices that will become habits of a lifetime. This TalkSheet is designed to help students learn to discipline and control their time so that they work well—and rest well, too. They can make a contribution to society and have a life that is productive by following God's principles.

OPENER

Have your students stand in the middle of the room. On a whiteboard or poster board, write the statement—I COULD GET ALL A'S IN SCHOOL. Ask the group to walk toward one end of the room if they agree with the statement, and the other end of the room if they disagree. Next, add to the statement by writing things like I COULD GET ALL A'S IN SCHOOL IF I WAS GIVEN $50 FOR EACH A I BROUGHT HOME. See how many move to the agree side. Keep upping the money amount until all the students agree with you're statement, or until you are offering $100,000 for each A. Point out that if the motivation is high enough, almost everyone will work hard to get straight A's. The thing that keeps many of people from doing what they're capable of is their own laziness.

THE DISCUSSION, BY NUMBERS

1. Ask the group to share their definitions of laziness. You may want to list their ideas on a whiteboard or poster board. Ask how they would rate themselves—are they productive or lazy?

2. Discuss these acts of laziness and their consequences. Point out that people form habits easily when they're young. But these habits can lead to worse results when they get older. What could happen if someone formed a permanent habit of the items listed? What worse outcomes could occur?

3. Take some time to talk about these verses. What do they say about an industrious man? What about the ant? Point out that an ant doesn't wait to be told what to do, but takes the initiative to accomplish what needs to be done. How can your kids apply these verses to their lives today?

4. Discuss the situation of the lazy man. Should he be bailed out of trouble? Why or why not? Allow for debate, and don't try to force the whole group

to a consensus. What about a friend? Are those circumstances different? Why or why not?

5. Ask the group why most people feel better about themselves and their lives when they work hard. Point out that hard work has its own reward—the satisfaction that leads to a positive and healthy self-image.

6. Are your kids forming lazy habits? Challenge them to think about an area of their life that they'd like to change and practical things that they could do this. You may want to have some volunteer share their thoughts.

THE CLOSE

Encourage your students to be wise stewards of their time and energy. Explain to them that they only have one lifetime and that they can use it to its fullest or they can squander it. Point out that while television and video games may be fun, they can devour hours and even days of their lives with little practical return. Challenge them to pay their dues in hard work for anything—from playing the guitar to getting good grades—rather than thinking they will magically get the rewards for those things in the future.

MORE

- Challenge your kids to go on a media fast—to give up the TV, the computer, and video games for one week. Encourage those kids throughout the week by phone calls or a postcard and at your next meeting, see how many were able to achieve the goal and how they used their time. What was the hardest part about giving those things up? Ask them if their experience will make a difference in how they will approach their free time in the future. Why or why not?

- Point out to the group that there's a difference between being productive and going overboard. Today's society is stressed out. Some kids in middle school or junior high are going to school, playing sports, and even working. And look at some of their parents working 50-plus hours a week. Talk with your group about the importance of relaxation and rest, along with being productive. How can your kids find productive ways to relax, without being lazy?

HONESTY COUNTS!

1. Would you go to a doctor who cheated his or her way through medical school?
   Why or why not?

2. Check **three** of the following that you would consider to be the most dishonest.
   - ❏ Telling someone that your mom isn't home when she just doesn't want to come to the phone
   - ❏ Giving false information about yourself on an Internet chat room
   - ❏ Saying that you like your friend's haircut when you really don't
   - ❏ Keeping the extra change that you've accidentally been given
   - ❏ Telling someone that you're busy after he or she asks you out
   - ❏ Bootlegging or copying a CD or video for your own use
   - ❏ Spilling a secret about a friend that you promised to keep
   - ❏ Taking the blame for something you didn't do in order to help another person save face
   - ❏ Taking the credit for a report you copied from another source
   - ❏ Telling your parents that you're going to the mall and then go somewhere else

3. When you're dishonest or lying, what do you worry about most?

4. Check out **Proverbs 10:9**. Do you agree with what it says? Why or why not?

5. On a scale below, put an X on the spot that indicates how honest you think you are.

I'm totally honest all the time   I'm the epitome of dishonesty

6. Check out what the verses below have to say. Then draw a connecting line between each Bible verse and it's summarizing statement.

Exodus 23:1	A truthful person doesn't deceive.
Leviticus 19:11	Speak truthfully to each other.
Psalm 37:21	Do not steal.
Proverbs 14:5	If you borrow, be sure to repay.
Ephesians 4:25	Don't spread false stories.

HONESTY COUNTS! [integrity—Proverbs 10]

THIS WEEK

The integrity of young teens is challenged—and compromised—daily. Will they be true to their word? Will they cheat at sports, games, or schoolwork? The battle to live a life of integrity never ends. Naturally, God sets high standards for integrity. But as high as they are, they are achievable and rewarding—especially when living with integrity becomes a habit.

OPENER

Play a few rounds of Balderdash. In this adapted version of the board game Beyond Balderdash, make a list of nonsense, very obscure words—but real words nonetheless (just look in a dictionary). A few examples from Dictionary.com (www.dictionary.com) might be—

- Coquette—a woman who flirts with a man
- Defenestration—an act of throwing someone or something out of a window.
- Doppelganger—a ghostly double.
- Fop—a man who is much concerned with his appearance.
- Restate—to move like a reptile; slither.
- Triskaidekaphobia—fear of the number 13.

You can either play as a large group or split your group up into small groups of 4 or 5 people per group. A player in each group begins by choosing a word from the categories, including words, people, objects, or any other one you want to include. All of the other players then write down a bluff, false answer to the word in the hopes of fooling each other. Shuffle the real answer in with all of the other players' phony answers and read each one aloud. A group scores points for guessing the real answer—and for also duping their peers into believing their answer is correct. Each person's task is to create a false definition for the word. Encourage your kids to try to make it sound realistic—and to be creative.

Afterwards, vote with your group for who made up the most believable, yet false definition for a word.

THE DISCUSSION, BY NUMBERS

1. Let your group point out the obvious—why they wouldn't trust a doctor who cheated through medical school. Throw in a few more examples, such as a president who lied to get into office, an athlete who set a world record while using illegal drugs, or a police officer who took bribes from rich crooks. Point out that honesty is one of the pillars of society because trust between people is essential.

2. Which of these items are the most dishonest? Which ones aren't really dishonest? Let your kids defend their ideas and decide as a group, under which situations one of these would be considered completely dishonest. You'll probably have some disagreement here—every situation noted doesn't necessarily have a black-and-white answer.

3. What is the downside of being dishonest? What problems or consequences come from frequently lying? Most liars, cheaters, promise breakers, and thieves live in fear that they will be caught or discovered—and later may feel extremely guilty

4. How did your kids summarize this verse? Do they agree or disagree with what it says? Why? Take some time to discuss how this verse applies to your kids today.

5. How honest do your kids think they are? Are they more to the left or to the right? Do any of them formed bad habits that have left them feeling dishonest? Point out that your kids aren't alone—nobody is perfect when it comes to maintaining integrity. In fact, if any of them have rated themselves as perfect, they're probably being dishonest with themselves!

6. You may want to read these verses as a group and summarize what each passage says. Point out that God lays out the standards for integrity. He is willing to forgive all shortcomings, but he wants honesty to become the habit of their lives.

THE CLOSE

Most junior high or middle schoolers know that honesty really is the best policy—even when it's painful. Take some time to talk about the pros and cons of honesty—why do some people think it's easier to lie? Why is it sometimes more hurtful or harder to tell the truth? Why is dishonesty promoted in culture sometime? And why do dishonest people get away with so much? Take some time to talk about these and some other issues with your group.

MORE

- Where do your kids see dishonesty in the media? You may want to bring in a few clips of a few movies or TV shows. What do these clips deal with? What are the causes and consequences of lying? Are these examples of big lies or little ones—and is there a difference in these? Challenge your kids to think about these questions through out the week.
- Ask your kids to look at some of the following verses from Proverbs on honesty—11:1, 11:3, 11:8, 12:5, 12:13, 12:19, 12:22, 14:5, 14:25, 16:13, 20:7, 20:10, 20:17, 20:21, 21:3, 21:6, 28:18, and 28:23. What do these proverbs say about the virtue of honesty? And how can your kids apply these verses in their lives today?

WATCH YOUR WORDS

1. What do you think it means to "put your foot in your mouth"?

   Have you ever "put your foot in your mouth"? What happened?

2. Check out **Proverbs 10:32**. What grade (A, B, C, D, or F) would you give your lips when it comes to saying the right things at the right time?

3. What do you think would be appropriate to say to each of the people below?
   A friend who just had a relative die?

   A person who is depressed or discouraged?

   A brother or sister who is lonely?

   A person who is very angry?

   A friend who has been dumped by a boyfriend or girlfriend?

   Your teammate who fumbled the ball on the crucial play?

4. When is joking around with someone okay and when can it be harmful?

5. Read each of these proverbs and then, in your own words, write the advice that each verse gives.
   Psalm 141:3
   Proverbs 12:18
   Proverbs 15:1
   Proverbs 15:4
   Proverbs 15:23
   Proverbs 29:11

WATCH YOUR WORDS

THIS WEEK

Words can sometimes be brutal. Teenagers—like adults—can say the wrong thing at the wrong time, whether they mean it or not. This TalkSheet is designed to help your students explore what to say, how to say it, and when to say nothing at all.

OPENER

Bring paper, markers, glue sticks, and a number of magazines and newspapers. Let your kids pick a pictures to cut out. Then ask them to come up with a humorous, silly, or random sentence to paste as a word balloon on the photo. You may want to have your kids paste their pictures and word balloons to sheets of poster board or tape them on the wall. When everyone has finished, let them look at the word balloons and enjoy some laughs. Move on to the lesson by telling your students that while what they have done may be funny and fictitious, people often say things just as silly or strange in real life. Tell them that they will be discussing the idea of using speech that fits the occasion.

THE DISCUSSION, BY NUMBERS

1. What does this mean to your kids? Ask them what it means—and feels— to say the wrong thing at the wrong time. Have any of them done this? What happened and how did they feel?

2. What grade did your kids give themselves? Are they proud of these grades or not? What grade would your group give teenagers in general? How would God feel about their grade and what do they think he'd say to your group members?

3. What would your group members say in teach of these situations? Make a list of their responses on a whiteboard or poster board. Would any of these responses qualify as being the wrong thing to say at the wrong time? Why or why not?

4. Many young people joke around and make fun of each other, most often in good-nature. But sometimes teenagers can become very cruel, even ganging up to rip someone to shreds. Have the students share their views on the limits to joking, when it can backfire, and when it can become hurtful.

5. Ask for a few of the group members to share their paraphrases of these proverbs. Point out the principles behind appropriate speech—people are called to be kind and gentle with their words, people should know when to say something, and people have a responsibility to keep their angry and harsh words under control. Does these proverbs apply to your kids' lives today? If so, how?

THE CLOSE

Summarize the points that have been made during the discussion. It takes wisdom to know what to say, when to say it, and when not to say anything at all. If you have time and think it's appropriate for your group, ask a few volunteers to role-play the situations described in question 4. Did these people say the right things at the right time? Why or why not? Be careful not to let the group criticize the others to harshly. Sometimes it's hard to know what to say in certain situations. Challenge your kids to think wisely through their actions and words—and to think about the consequences of their words.

MORE

● Ask your students to think of one person who they've probably not responded to in the best way. Have they hurt the other person? Do they have any regrets about their words? Encourage your kids to come clean with that person during the week. Or to think of how they might handle that person—and their words—in the future.

● Words can be brutal—sometimes too harsh. Verbal abuse is an unfortunate reality in the lives of teenagers and families today. Like physical or sexual abuse, destructive words leave wounds that last a lifetime. You may have some kids in your group who are—or have friends who are—victims of verbal or emotional abuse. For more information on this issue, visit Child Help USA (www.child-helpusa.org) or the American Humane Association (www.americanhumane.org). And encourage your kids to find an adult, school counselor, teacher, or pastor to talk with.

WINDOW TO THE SOUL

1. A person might be described as being made up of two layers—the shell on the outside and the being on the inside. Which of the following items deal with the **outside of a person (S)** and which deal with the **inside contents (C)**? Which deal with **both (B)**?

___ Strength   ___ Friendliness   ___ Ugliness
___ Courage   ___ Patience   ___ Honesty
___ Faith   ___ Self-control   ___ Agility
___ Beauty   ___ Muscles   ___ Imagination
___ Creativity ___ Generosity   ___ Humor
___ Kindness   ___ Godliness   ___ Intelligence
___ Style   ___ Attractiveness

2. What do you think the average person is most concerned about—his or her outside appearance or inner self? Why?

3. Check out **Proverbs 11:22**. Which of the following do you think best describes the symbolism used in the passage?
   - ❏ a. Pretty women make better wives than pigs.
   - ❏ b. A person may have beauty on the outside, but foolishness on the inside is a waste.
   - ❏ c. Don't waste gold on a dirty pig when you can use it as a wedding ring.
   - ❏ d. A woman with no discretion will hang around with pigs.
   - ❏ e. Pigs and people without sound judgment are the same.
   - ❏ f. Beautiful people should have wise judgment and pigs shouldn't wear jewelry.

4. What do you think of these statements? Do you think each one is **T (true)** or **F (false)**?
   ___ Most people put more effort into how they look than who they are.
   ___ A beautiful person can also be ugly.
   ___ A person who is handsome or pretty will get further in life than someone who isn't.
   ___ A person who is attractive on the outside is usually attractive on the inside as well.

5. Check out the following passages and in your words, write down the qualities of true beauty described in these verses.
   Matthew 5:8
   Galatians 5:22-23
   Ephesians 4:22-24

From *Junior High-Middle School TalkSheets Psalms and Proverbs—Updated!* by Rick Bundschuh and Tom Finley. Permission to reproduce this page granted only for use in the buyer's own youth group. www.YouthSpecialties.com

WINDOW TO THE SOUL [inner beauty—Proverbs 11]

THIS WEEK

Young teens are bombarded by a world of attractive and desirable images. They know that appearance is important and spend a lot of their time primping and worrying about how they look. But many don't recognize the need to put at least an equal amount of time and effort into developing their inner character. The writer of Proverbs equates a jewelry-wearing pig (an animal unclean to the Jews) with a person who is attractive on the outside but ugly on the inside. This TalkSheet offers an opportunity to talk with your students about working on their character, their spiritual lives, and their personalities with the same fervor that they work on their outside appearance.

OPENER

Try this one with your group—put a mirror, facing up, in a large paper bag or shoebox. Now play a round of 20 questions with your group. What do they think is inside the bag? You'll get all kinds of questions—but the point is that the thing inside the bag is a reflection of the person looking in. If you look inside the bag at the mirror, you'll see yourself. Answer the questions as if each kid is looking inside the bag at the mirror. When they've given up, let them take turns looking inside the bag—at themselves. How ugly or pretty do they think they are when they look inside? Are they pleased with what they see? Why or why not? Now how pleased would they be if they actually looked inside themselves? What reflection would they see there?

THE DISCUSSION, BY NUMBERS

1. Ask your students to explore which of these attributes are external, internal, or both. They may debate and disagree on some of these. Discuss which can be both outward and inner attributes, such as strength, attractiveness, beauty, and ugliness.

2. If the group is honest, they'll probably admit that the average person worries more about his or her outside package. What makes people feel that the outside is more important than the inside? Point out the importance that the media puts on outer beauty and looks. How can this hurt a person's self-esteem?

3. How did your kids interpret this verse? The correct answers are b and e. Point out that a pig was considered an unclean animal to the Hebrew writer who wrote these proverbs.

4. What did your kids think of these questions? Talk about each one that they agreed and disagreed with. Ask the group how long they think outer beauty will last as they get older—until age 30? 50? 80? Forever? In contrast, how long does inner beauty last? According to God, it lasts a lot longer than outer beauty—and it's much more important, too.

5. Work the your group to describe these biblical qualities for inner beauty in their own words. You may want to ask how these qualities can be seen in people today and invite them to affirm such qualities that they see in one another. Point out how these can get better with age—unlike physical beauty!

THE CLOSE

Point out just how consumed with looks society is. Some people think it's sickening. And although you won't dissuade your kids from spending time in front of the mirror, you can remind them that it is entirely possible to be drop-dead gorgeous person, but have an utterly unattractive character. Give them the straightforward fact that God looks only at the heart and—because the body is a shell—who people are will last forever. That's why God wants people to invest in their inner qualities. Brainstorm with some ways that your kids can work on their character—or at least how they can balance it out with the time they spend on their appearances. Challenge them to think about making a commitment to spend more time with God during the week, to improve a friendship or family relationship, to volunteer their extra time, or something else.

MORE

● Using the discussion from question 1, you may want to make a two-column list of the characteristics of external beauty and inner beauty. Then compare these two lists and decide with your group how concerned people their age are about the characteristics in each column. Why are people so focused on their outside selves, but yet worried about the violence, vulgarity, and anger in the world today? Why do they think so many girls their age have become victims of eating disorders and depression? Give your kids time to think about these and other questions that they might have.

● Outer beauty isn't a bad thing—in fact, it's essential for a healthy self-esteem and having good hygiene. The important thing is that the kids feel good about themselves and accept them as they are now. Ask your kids to think of one thing that they can do during the week, over the next month, or even year, to improve the way they feel about themselves. Do some of them want to stop doing something...like biting their nails? Maybe some want to set some exercise goals or stop eating oodles of calories in after school snacks. Whatever it is, challenge your kids to think about how they can be contented with themselves—as they are. You may want to spend some more time talking about God's views of beauty and health.

GIVE OR TAKE

1. **Who was the last person that you bought a gift for with your own money?**

   Mom   Friend   Grandparent
   Dad   Girlfriend or boyfriend   Self
   Brother   Teacher   No one
   Sister   Pastor   Other—
   Neighbor   Aunt or uncle

2. **How would you complete this statement in your own words?**

   It's said that giving is better than receiving.
   If I had a choice, I'd rather—

3. **What is one gift that you'd like to give to someone if you could afford it?**
   Who would you give it to and why?

4. **Check the three best ways to be a giver, in your opinion.**

   ❏ Do someone a favor.
   ❏ Spend time playing with a sibling.
   ❏ Pray for someone.
   ❏ Lend a hand.
   ❏ Tutor someone in school.
   ❏ Buy something for someone.
   ❏ Put money in the church offering.

   ❏ Give money to a charity or other organization.
   ❏ E-mail an encouragement to a friend or classmate.
   ❏ Spend time with a lonely senior citizen.
   ❏ Say something kind to someone.
   ❏ Other—

5. **Read Proverbs 11:24. What doesn't appear to make sense in this verse?**
   What could the answer be?

6. **Match these passages with what they have to say about being a giver.**

   Proverbs 22:9   People should give with a cheerful attitude.
   Matthew 6:1-4   People who are generous will be blessed by God.
   Acts 20:35   People should give quietly and secretly.
   2 Corinthians 9:7   Giving really is better than receiving.

From *Junior High-Middle School TalkSheets Psalms and Proverbs—Updated!* by Rick Bundschuh and Tom Finley. Permission to reproduce this page granted only for use in the buyer's own youth group. www.YouthSpecialties.com

77

GIVE OR TAKE [generosity — Proverbs 11]

THIS WEEK

Junior highers and middle schoolers sometimes totter on the fence between being childish takers and mature, generous givers. They can develop an attitude toward giving that will affect them the rest of their lives.

OPENER

You may want to open by writing a few situations like these (feel free to make up your own) on 3 x 5 cards or pieces of paper. Read each situation to the group or have volunteers read them to the group. What would your kids do in each situation?

⇨ Your neighbor won't be home on Halloween. She doesn't want to disappoint any kids who come to her house to trick or treat, so she buys a few bags of candy and pours them in a box outside her house. Above the box she places a sign that says, "Please take one!" Will you take one? Or will you scoop out a whole bunch of candies?

⇨ You know that a friend is going to get you a gift for Christmas. She (or he) isn't a super-close friend and you don't have any extra allowance to buy her (or him) a gift. What will you do? Do you think your friend is expecting a present in return? What if you were the friend? How would you respond then?

⇨ It's your birthday and you know you're going to get a present. Your mom (or dad) comes home from work with a small birthday cake—but no gift. She (or he) says that money is tight and that you'll get a present after the next paycheck. How will you respond? How would you feel if you were your mom (or dad)?

⇨ You've been babysitting your little brother a lot after school, before your parents get home from work. They haven't been paying you and you're starting to get mad. Then one night they give you a gift certificate to any store that you want. How do you feel now? Would you continue to baby sit your brother, knowing that you may not get rewarded again?

THE DISCUSSION, BY NUMBERS

1. Who have your kids bought gifts for? Some of your kids have a lot of their own money and buy a lot of stuff on their own. Others never buy anything for themselves. Your point isn't to judge kids for having their own money or not—but to talk about how it feels to give something after you've worked hard to buy it.

2. Make a list of your kids' responses on a poster board or whiteboard. Would they rather receive or give?

3. Who would your kids give the gift of their dreams to and why? Make a list of the gifts they'd give. Then ask them how easy it'd be to afford a gift like this in their lifetime.

4. Point out that being a giving person involves more than giving just material gifts. A giving person gives in all areas of life. Many of the things they give are priceless—such as encouraging friends, volunteering time that could be spent doing something else, and showing love to others. Is it more easy or difficult to give material gifts or other gifts?

5. What seems strange about this verse? Take some time to talk about God's strange (but functional!) economy—to give is to gain, to die is to live, to be last is to be first. How can these principles apply to the lives of your kids today?

6. What do your kids think it means to live a life of godly generosity? You may want to re-read these verses with the group and talk more specifically about each one. How can your kids apply these attributes in their own lives? Encourage them to give specific examples.

THE CLOSE

Wrap up with your kids by asking what the benefits are of being a giver. How are others affected by their generosity? How does giving change the person who gives? What happens when giving people give too much? Or when the takers take too much? Talk about balancing giving with taking. Then challenge your group to follow up on the ideas they brainstormed in question 6. Is there something that you as a group can do together?

MORE

● You may want to—and if your kids are interested—pick names anonymously for secret supporters. Then for a week, a month, or more, these people can secretly support and encourage each other by giving small gifts, a letter, or even just prayer. Follow up with your group and ask them how it felt to give and to receive. What was easier or harder? And how did they feel when they gave and didn't receive (or vice versa?). Why is it hard to give unconditionally?

● You may want to talk about the paradox of giving within a society like the United States. How can your kids survive in this culture and maintain or develop a giving nature? What can they do to keep themselves and others from getting caught up in wanting it all?

DID YOU HEAR?

1. If you had a **secret** that you wanted to tell someone, who would you tell?

   - ❏ Friend
   - ❏ Parent
   - ❏ Youth pastor
   - ❏ Boyfriend or girlfriend
   - ❏ Teacher
   - ❏ Brother or sister
   - ❏ Grandparent

   - ❏ Stranger in an on-line chat room
   - ❏ Coach
   - ❏ School counselor
   - ❏ The class gossip
   - ❏ Nobody
   - ❏ Other—

2. Have you ever had someone you trust spill a secret about you?

   If yes, how did it make you feel?

   How did it change your relationship with the person you told the secret to?

3. For which of the situations below would you break the confidence of a friend and tell some one else?
   - ❏ Your friend tells you the he or she likes someone.
   - ❏ Your friend says she is pregnant.
   - ❏ Your friend confesses to cheating on the English final.
   - ❏ Your friend tells you something they're ashamed of doing.
   - ❏ Your friend tells you that an uncle is sexually abusing him or her.
   - ❏ Your friend confesses to experimenting with drugs.
   - ❏ Your friend admits to considering running away from home.
   - ❏ Your friend confides in you about being HIV positive.
   - ❏ Your friend tells you he or she is thinking about suicide.

4. Read the passages below and summarize each verse in your own words.
   Proverbs 11:13
   Proverbs 17:9
   Proverbs 20:19
   Ephesians 4:29

DID YOU HEAR? [gossip—Proverbs 11, 17, 20]

THIS WEEK

Some young people have a lot of secrets. And for some, nothing is as fun as leaking a juicy tidbit from somebody's life. Gossip is a national pastime in their culture. Adults, young people, and the media seem to revel in gossip. Although sometimes interesting, it can destroy reputations and tear apart friendships. This TalkSheet will help your group discover that only some things need to be shared with others, and that keeping a confidence will strengthen friendships and build trust between people.

OPENER

There's no better example of gossip than the media tabloid. You may want to purchase a couple of these at any grocery store or drug store and select a few short articles to read to your group. Ask your students to vote on which stories they think are true and which they think are false. What makes a story believable? Why or why not? And why do people buy into these stories and false lies about others? Discuss what sells those tabloids. You may want to rewrite one of the stories using the names of some of the young people in your group, then talk about what it would feel like to have these kind of stories written about people.

For Internet tabloid sites (so you don't have to be seen buying one!), check out Tabloids.com (http://4tabloids.4anything.com), the National Enquirer (www.nationalenquirer.com), or Star Magazine (www.starmagazine.com).

THE DISCUSSION, BY NUMBERS

1. Who would your kids most likely to trust with a secret and why? Why is this person trustworthy and how well do you think the person would be able to hold the information in confidence?

2. How did your kids feel when this situation happened to them? Have a few willing students share what happened to them and how the situation affected the friendship (no names, please!). Has this situation changed the way your kids handle the secrets of others?

3. Go over which secrets a real friend should absolutely not keep (suicide threats or sexual abuse, for example). Be prepared for a lot of disagreement on some of these issues. Point out the potential harm that comes from not telling someone else if a friend is keeping a harmful secret.

4. Have a few willing students share their phrases (being trustworthy, betraying a confidence, promoting love, and so on). Talk to your students about the impact that breaking a confidence has on friendships, trust, and their integrity as Christians. You may want to summarize each verse as a group and write each one on a poster board or whiteboard.

THE CLOSE

Point out to your students that people human beings are strange creatures—people love the tidbits of scandal and the lure of knowing something that others would rather keep private. It causes people to be focused on anything but the essentials of being honest, truthful, and real with others—and with God. Encourage your kids to keep a careful ear open for what they hear and to become discerning listeners as well. They can choose what to believe and what not to believe. And they carry the responsibility of what to remember and pass on to others. How would they want others to handle their deepest secrets?

MORE

● You may have some kids in your group who are holding some secrets that are eating them inside—possibly an abusive parent, failing grades, the lure of drugs or sex, or more. These are real issues that need real attention. Pay close attention to your kids during this discussion and let the group know how crucial it is to talk with a trusted adult. For more information check out www.YouthSpecialties.com for more links to sites on issues in teen's lives including rape, abuse, pregnancy, suicide and more. Or see TalkSheets Soul Pollution (53), The Perfect Parent (31), and Is God Keeping Score? (19) for more links and discussion items.

● God isn't a fool. He knows what is going on in the lives of your kids and their friends. You may want to talk about these psalms more in depth. How do your kids feel knowing that God knows their secrets—before they even tell him? Challenge them to get real with God and bring their fears and concerns to him. He's their greatest, most trusted friend—whether they know it or not.

LIVID OR LET GO

1. Think of the last time you lost your temper. Check the box below that most closely describes that situation.

   I lost my temper with—
   - ❏ A sibling
   - ❏ A teacher
   - ❏ A parent
   - ❏ A friend
   - ❏ A kid at school
   - ❏ A pet
   - ❏ A member of the opposite sex
   - ❏ A stranger

   - ❏ I got mad about—
   - ❏ What somebody said
   - ❏ What somebody did to me
   - ❏ What somebody should have done, but didn't
   - ❏ What somebody did to another person
   - ❏ I don't remember, but it made me mad
   - ❏ Other—

2. What do you think is the difference between **being angry** and **losing your temper**?

3. Rate the ways people react when they lose their temper, from the **worst (1)** to the **harmless (10)**.
   - ___ Slam doors or throw things
   - ___ Scream and yell
   - ___ Get mad at people who have nothing to do with the situation
   - ___ Clench fists, grind teeth, bulge eyes, and breathe hard
   - ___ Say hurtful words
   - ___ Cry
   - ___ Hit, slap, scratch, and push
   - ___ Destroy property, commit crimes
   - ___ Use foul language and curses
   - ___ Do nothing and keep it inside

4. Do you think a temper is **controllable**?

5. Look up one of the following passages and re-write it in your own words.

   Proverbs 12:16
   Proverbs 15:1
   Proverbs 15:18
   Proverbs 16:32

   Proverbs 19:19
   Ephesians 4:26
   James 1:19

From *Junior High-Middle School TalkSheets Psalms and Proverbs—Updated!* by Rick Bundschuh and Tom Finley. Permission to reproduce this page granted only for use in the buyer's own youth group. www.YouthSpecialties.com

81

LIVID OR LET GO

[c o n t r o l l i n g   y o u r   t e m p e r — P r o v e r b s   1 2 ,   1 5 ,   1 6 ,   1 9]

THIS WEEK

Some people have tempers that are worse than others. Some people handle their anger in different ways. Teenagers often to see tempers flare in adults who should have brought them under control long ago. This TalkSheet will give your students an opportunity to examine how they react to disturbing situations, and to discuss what kind of behavior and self-control they should strive for.

OPENER

Set up three corners of the room—one for short-fused people, one for even-tempered people, and one for very easygoing people. Tell the group that after you read a situation, they should to go to the corner that would represent how they would handle the pressure. Situations you can suggest include omeone insulting you, someone insulting your mother, someone beating up your friend, someone beating up your five-year-old brother, someone breaking something and then blaming you, someone cussing you out, or someone slapping around a person in a wheelchair. Make a longer list if you'd like and include situations as serious as you'd like.

Or ask your group to bring in examples of songs that express anger or rebellion. Play the song or read the lyrics and talk about what the anger is and how the person could deal with it. What does the song say about anger? What is the singer angry about? How do they handle their anger? Is it good or bad?

THE DISCUSSION, BY NUMBERS

1. When did your kids lose their tempers and what happened when they did? Take some time for them to share their experiences. Why is it easier for some people to loose their temper than for others?

2. Talk about the difference between being angry and losing your temper. Where is the fine liney-ou're your kids? Jesus was angry at times, too, and seemed to lose his temper once (Matthew 21:10-13). You may want to read these verses to your kids. Is it ever appropriate for your kids to loose their tempers? Why or why not?

3. How did your kids rank these reactions? You may want to rank them as a group. Which reaction is the most harmful or dangerous? Why? Point out how much damage can be done when people blow up in anger. How do your kids react to other people who lose their temper?

4. Take a poll of your group to see how they answered this question. Challenge them with the question of whether or not people can control

their tempers at all. Is there a point where a person can lose his or her ability to control themself? If so, when?

5. Take some time to talk about the Bible's teaching on anger. You may want to read these verses again as a group and discuss how a person can attempt to calm and control his or her anger.

THE CLOSE

Anger is a human emotion—it's okay to feel irritated and angry from time to time. But controlling anger means having self-control. Some people lack the self-control to stop themselves before they blow it and hurt someone. Point out that self-control is a fruit of the spirit. Help for dealing with anger isn't too far away. God gives peace and he gives self-control. Challenge your kids to try the ten-second anger test. If they feel irritated, silently stop and count to ten—slowly. Then think about how they're reacting. Are they willing to let God give them self control—or will they go ahead blow their lid?

MORE

● Some of your kids may experience anger and rage first hand. You may have kids in your group who have been hurt, yelled at, or hit by their friends, siblings or parents—or maybe have seen a sibling or parent get hit. If you sense situations of physical abuse, take note of it, encourage your kids to talk with an adult, and to stop the abuse now. Explain to your group that under no circumstances can a parent beat a child or another family member. For more information on domestic violence and abuse, check out Child Help USA (www.child-helpusa.org) or the American Humane Association (www.americanhumane.org), The Family Violence Prevention Fund (www.fvpf.org), or Christians In Recovery (www.christians-in-recovery.com).

● What other characters in the Bible dealt with anger? You may want to break your group up into smaller groups and let them find an example of anger in the Bible. A few of these include Job—who didn't get angry with God, Jesus—who got angry in the Temple, Judas Iscariot—who got so angry at himself that he killed himself, and even God himself—who got angry and destroyed Sodom and Gomorrah. Talk about these and more examples with your group and how this relates to their lives today. What lessons on temper can be learned from these characters?

ONE TRUE THING

1. Do you **agree** or **disagree** with this statement? Why?
It doesn't matter what you believe as long as you're sincere.

2. List something that you once believed was true, but now you don't believe is true.

3. How many of your friends would agree with the following statements?
A (all of them), M (most of them), M (many of them), or N (none of them)?
___ If it's in the paper or on TV, it must be true.
___ If it makes sense, it must be true.
___ If you think or believe it, it must be true.
___ If your teacher says it, it must be true.
___ If everyone else believes it, it must be true.
___ If it's in the Bible, it must be true.
___ If it's on the Internet, it must be true.
___ If your parents believe it, it must be true.

4. Which of the items below do you think is most important to be right about?
- ❑ which toothpaste gives sex appeal
- ❑ what kind of car is better
- ❑ who is trustworthy
- ❑ which songs to download
- ❑ what basketball team is best
- ❑ how to find eternal life
- ❑ which video game is the best
- ❑ which church to go to
- ❑ what friends to hang out with
- ❑ what kind of music is best
- ❑ what brand of clothing to buy
- ❑ how to know what is right and what is wrong

5. Check out these passages and summarize the meaning of each one in your own words.
Proverbs 14:12
John 14:6

ONE TRUE THING [God's truth—Proverbs 14]

THIS WEEK

Most young people—including many within the church—would quickly affirm that it doesn't matter what people believe as long as they sincerely believe it. This faulty line of thinking flies in the face of Christ's words proclaiming himself to be the only source of life-giving truth (John 14:6). This perspective can also foster a mood of false tolerance. Racism isn't acceptable simply because some sincerely believe in it. Kids need to know that truth is more than mere sincerity. This TalkSheet helps them probe into the blurred thinking of the world and compare it with the teaching of the Bible.

OPENER

Do your students know why Native Americans were called Indians by the early European explorers? The reason is that Columbus thought he had landed in India. He didn't know that he had discovered a new continent. Columbus sincerely believed that these dark-skinned people were from India. But his sincerity didn't change the fact that he was wrong—and his error is why Native Americans are mistakenly referred to as Indians to this day. What does this say about sincerity and one's beliefs?

Kids today live in a postmodern world. Many are taught to believe anything they want to. You may want to ask your kids what the kids at their schools believe. What religions or beliefs do your kids know or hear about in society, in their schools, and from their friends? Which ones do they disagree or argue with? How does it make them feel knowing that someone can believe whatever they want, whether it's true or not? Does this make truth more important or less important?

THE DISCUSSION, BY NUMBERS

1. What do your kids think about sincerity and truth? Take a group poll to see what they think and let them defend their thoughts and opinions with each other.

2. Ask your kids to share some things they used to believe in. You may want to make a list of these on a whiteboard or poster board. What changed those beliefs? What does your group think about those who continue to believe in things like folk tales or superstitions?

3. What sources do people tend to believe? What makes some of these sources credible—or not? What sources would Chrsitians turst more than others and why? Challenge them to think about the trustworthiness of the sources of information they rely on.

4. Ask for some volunteers to share their answers. You may want to rank them in order of importance with your group. Which five do your kids think are most important to be right about and why? What could happen to people who think they are smart enough to make their own way in life?

5. Read these verses with your group and discuss the summaries that they wrote. What are the implications of these passages for your kids today? What options do they give to people who feel that whatever they sincerely believe is legitimate?

THE CLOSE

The ultimate truth is found in the Bible. Sincerity can deceptively seem like honesty, when in fact, it's not. The teachings of the Bible are their source for truth—they are solid, even if people find them uncomfortable. Challenge your students to think carefully about the various so-called truths that they hear and to compare them with the one true thing—the Word of God. How does knowing the truth make them feel? And are they willing to share this truth with those around them?

MORE

- With your group, go around the circle and ask each person to say something that they believe sincerely about, other than the truth of the Bible. For example, one could believe sincerely that it's essential to get enough sleep. Have your students share these with each other and make a master list of these truths. Then rate these truths on a scale of 1 to 10 (1 being "everyone in the world believes this" and 10 being "there's hardly anyone who believes this"). How would the world rate the truth of God and his son Jesus? Where do your kids think society stands with the sincere belief in Christ? And are they willing to help others see the truth? Brainstorm with your group some ways to make this happen and to jumpstart your kids to getting the word out.

- Do your kids want to know or understand more about the truth? Bring the Bible to the level they understand. Check out the Wild Truth Bible series (Youth Specialties). This line of lessons and student journals give straight answers to who God is and what loving him is all about. For more information and other resources, check out www.YouthSpecialties.com.

CHEER UP!

1. Circle two things that would make you **feel better** if you were feeling down.

   A hilarious movie

   Reading a good book

   Some time alone

   Hearing your favorite song

   Getting an e-mail from a friend

   Hanging out with friends

   Eating your favorite dessert

   Getting a hug from a parent or friend

   Being able to stay home from school

   Getting a phone call from a friend

   Hearing a good joke

   Getting a card from a friend or family member

   Getting flowers from your boyfriend or girlfriend

   Other—

2. Do you think that cheerfulness is contagious?

3. Check out these statements—do you think each one is **T (true)** or **F (false)**?

   ___ You can make something more tolerable by having a cheerful outlook.

   ___ Having a cheerful disposition is something you're born with.

   ___ Cheerful people don't have any problems.

   ___ A person can learn to be more cheerful.

   ___ Being cheerful is unrealistic.

   ___ Cheerfulness and being a clown are the same thing.

   ___ Cheerful people have more friends than others.

4. Read **Proverbs 15:30** and **17:22**. Based on these verses, what would you say to someone who was constantly in a bad mood?

5. Select **two** of the scenarios below and describe how you could react cheerfully in each situation (use the back of this paper to write your responses).

   • The girl or guy that you really liked is now dating someone else.

   • Your mom or dad announced that you have to babysit your little sister (or brother).

   • Your team lost the big playoff game.

   • Your mom and dad filed for divorce.

   • The computer crashed when you were in the middle of writing your report.

   • Your older sister is in a particularly nasty mood.

   • You got a bad grade on an important test.

   • You've been grounded longer than you think you should've been.

   • Your teacher embarrassed you in class.

   • Your friend got asked to the dance and you didn't.

   • Your coach pulled you from the starting line-up.

   • A friend borrowed your favorite shirt and returned it with a huge stain.

CHEER UP! [cheerfulness—Proverbs 15, 17]

THIS WEEK

Young people are learning that their attitudes can help or hurt them. One of the most helpful attitudes they can develop is cheerfulness. Those with an upbeat, cheerful outlook (without being annoying) tend to be well liked—and since teens often feel disliked by their peers, this comes as good news. Cheerfulness improves relationships with parents, family, and friends, and reduces some of the trauma of the teenage years. This TalkSheet will help your students see that a cheerful attitude—even about difficult situations—can make all the difference in the world.

OPENER

You might want to start off by showing a few clips of movies that your kids have seen in recent movies. If you ask them to bring some examples in, be sure to view them beforehand to check the content. After showing these, ask the group how humor and cheerfulness played into the story or the situation. How did the character use humor or cheerfulness to deal with their problem or situation? And was it appropriate? Was the result a good one and did others appreciate the humor?

Or you may want to share some funny (and clean!) jokes. Have a few stories and jokes prepared to throw in yourself—you can find tons of them on the Internet by searching with the keyword "jokes." Maybe some kids in your group have some jokes to throw in too. Afterwards, note with your group how the atmosphere of the meeting changes when humor and cheerfulness are injected.

THE DISCUSSION, BY NUMBERS

1. What would make your kids feel better when they're in a downer mood? Encourage them to add their own examples. Why do some of these things cheer people up? If so, does it cheer them up temporarily or for a long time?

2. Do your kids agree that cheerfulness is contagious? Have them explain their answers. Then ask if this contagious cheerfulness is a good thing and what makes it contagious. Example include someone getting them into a laughing mood. At what point can cheefulness be annoying or inappropriate (for example, trying to make light of a bad situation, such as a death of a loved one)?

3. Did your kids agree or disagree with these statements? Discuss the nature of cheerfulness and cheerful people. Does a person learn to be cheerful—or are they born with it?

4. Read these verses with your group and summarize what they say. Based on these verses, what would your kids say to a person who was constantly negative or in a bad mood? How can your kids apply these verses to their lives today? Do they know someone who needs to apply these verses to their lives as well?

5. Have a few willing students share their responses. You may want to split your group up into smaller groups to discuss a few of these situations. What would be some probable solutions to these situations? Ask for some practical ways to show a positive and cheerful attitude, without going overboard. What are the results of such an attitude?

THE CLOSE

Humor and cheerfulness are good for the soul. Wrap up the session by talking about the benefits (both for themselves and others!) of developing a cheerful attitude and trusting God to work out things that are beyond their control. Point out that this doesn't mean going through life with their heads in the sand, but instead taking an hopeful outlook on life—knowing that everything is in the control of a loving God.

But some of your kids may be in situations in which a cheerful attitude can't fix the pain—such as a divorce in the family, an abusive situation, clinical depression, and more. Point out that cheerfulness can't fix problems and it certainly can't mend them. People in these situations need to seek out help and guidance from an adult, such as a school counselor, teacher, or pastor. If you sense any of these situations in your group, be sure to follow up with your kids—don't take any of these situations lightly.

MORE

● Hope is essential to having a cheerful attitude—it means having hope that things will work out for the best. You may want to have your kids look for other passages of scripture that deal with hope and assurance in God. What do these verses say about hope for the future and finding peace in God for their problems? What does the hope of eternal life mean for Christians today?

● You may want to plan a fun activity for your kids—something to give them a break from the norm and have fun (thus, the cheerfulness theme). It can be something simple like a pizza party, a night of bowling, a scavenger hunt, or something else. Point out that people can encourage each other and encourage cheerfulness among others.

HOW GREAT I AM

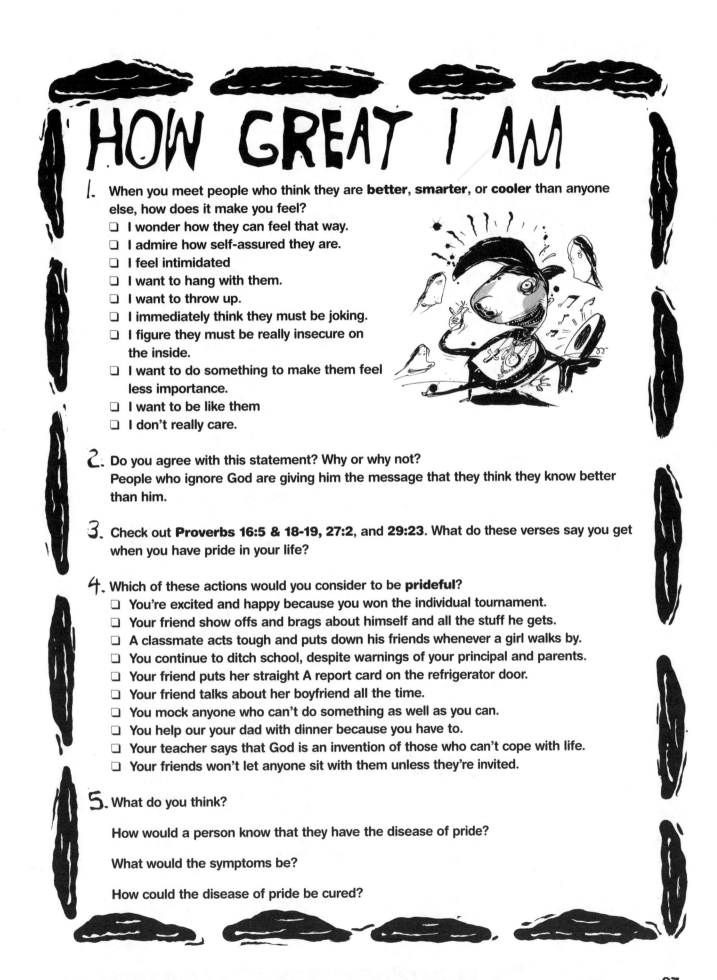

1. When you meet people who think they are **better**, **smarter**, or **cooler** than anyone else, how does it make you feel?
   - ❏ I wonder how they can feel that way.
   - ❏ I admire how self-assured they are.
   - ❏ I feel intimidated
   - ❏ I want to hang with them.
   - ❏ I want to throw up.
   - ❏ I immediately think they must be joking.
   - ❏ I figure they must be really insecure on the inside.
   - ❏ I want to do something to make them feel less importance.
   - ❏ I want to be like them
   - ❏ I don't really care.

2. Do you agree with this statement? Why or why not?
   People who ignore God are giving him the message that they think they know better than him.

3. Check out **Proverbs 16:5 & 18-19, 27:2**, and **29:23**. What do these verses say you get when you have pride in your life?

4. Which of these actions would you consider to be **prideful**?
   - ❏ You're excited and happy because you won the individual tournament.
   - ❏ Your friend show offs and brags about himself and all the stuff he gets.
   - ❏ A classmate acts tough and puts down his friends whenever a girl walks by.
   - ❏ You continue to ditch school, despite warnings of your principal and parents.
   - ❏ Your friend puts her straight A report card on the refrigerator door.
   - ❏ Your friend talks about her boyfriend all the time.
   - ❏ You mock anyone who can't do something as well as you can.
   - ❏ You help our your dad with dinner because you have to.
   - ❏ Your teacher says that God is an invention of those who can't cope with life.
   - ❏ Your friends won't let anyone sit with them unless they're invited.

5. What do you think?

   How would a person know that they have the disease of pride?

   What would the symptoms be?

   How could the disease of pride be cured?

HOW GREAT I AM [pride Proverbs—16, 27, 29]

THIS WEEK

Every person is prideful to one degree or another. Pride can mean bragging or self-glorification—but your teenagers need to understand that pride is also found hidden in other attitudes, like wanting to make fun of others or feeling that no one can tell them what to do. Pride is most destructive when it challenges God, and many young people do—passively. They simply ignore him, even while saying that they believe in him. The cure to pride is humility—the realization that people aren't any more special than anyone else and that people are all equal before God. This TalkSheet will help your students to define pride, to understand its destructive power in their lives, and to explore its cure.

OPENER

Start out by asking your kids to share an example of pride or to list all the words or phrases they think describe or reflect pride. A few examples might include—
* thinking you're better than someone else
* rubbing your good grades in someone else's face
* bragging to your best friend
* ignoring your mom when she says she needs your help

Write all of these examples and phrases on a whiteboard or poster board for the group to see. Then go through them with your group and rate them on a scale of 1 to 10 (1 being very prideful and 10 being not prideful at all). Then ask your group when pride becomes a bad thing. Where is the line between feeling good about yourself and being too proud? Why is pride harmful to relationships and friendships? Then jump into the TalkSheet discussion.

THE DISCUSSION, BY NUMBERS

1. How does it feel to interact with people who are prideful? Take a poll of your group to see what the most common response was. Why do teenagers react this way? Ask if your students think these people are even aware of their pride. Explain the difference between people who brag because they are insecure versus people who boast because they genuinely think they're superior.

2. How did your kids respond to this statement? What do they think about ignoring God? What are the consequences of ignoring God? You may want to ask your group to define pride and talk about subtle forms of pride such as resistance, stubbornness, and rebellion.

3. What do these verses say about pride? Discuss the results of sinful pride—both temporary and eternal. What is God's perspective on pride? How does pride affects Christians and how they reflect God to others?

4. Which actions do your students think are (or are not) prideful? Why or why not? Let your kids debate their opinions with each other. You may want to ask your kids to come up with a group definition of pride.

5. Have your young people share their symptoms of pride. Refer them back to the biblical examples—a haughty spirit, a boastful tongue, and an attitude of disdain. Point them also to the cure for pride—a lowly spirit, an attitude of humility, and a willingness to do without.

THE CLOSE

Point out to the group that pride puts distance between a person and God. Prideful people set themselves up as their own supreme authority—they become their own god. On the other hand, people who have the humility to obey God are blessed and rewarded by him. And those who have the humility to see others as worthy and valuable end up having more friends than those who are too prideful. Explain how Jesus dissolved the barriers of pride by eating with social outcasts, hanging out with so-called sinners, and picking common people for his disciples. How is pride affecting your kids? Have they hurt a friend, parent or God by being too prideful? How does it feel to be looked down upon by others?

MORE

● To bring this proverb closer to home, you may want to have your group rewrite it in their own words and then share examples about the behaviors mentioned. Then make copies of this rewritten proverb and e-mail it or pass it out to your kids. Encourage them to read it and think it through when they're dealing with issues of pride at school or at home.

● Sometimes being proud comes from the lack of accountability with others. Some parents don't notice the pride in their kids—others ignore it. Challenge your kids to hold themselves and others accountable to pride. You may want to talk about ways that your kids can hold themselves, their friends, parents, and others accountable against pride.

THERE FOR YOU

1. **What do you think? Are each of the things below E (easy) or D (difficult) for you?**
   ___ Making friends
   ___ Keeping friends for a long time
   ___ Becoming better friends with someone
   ___ Breaking apart a friendship
   ___ Being a good friend to others

2. **If you were able to download the perfect friend and select qualities on the Web site that are important to a friendship, which five of the following would you pick? Remember—only five!**

   - ❑ Similar interests
   - ❑ Loyal
   - ❑ Funny
   - ❑ Smart
   - ❑ Athletic
   - ❑ Able to keep secrets

   - ❑ Musical
   - ❑ Popular
   - ❑ Truthful
   - ❑ Spiritual
   - ❑ Trustworthy
   - ❑ Honest
   - ❑ Good-looking
   - ❑ Same age

   - ❑ Same race
   - ❑ Wealthy
   - ❑ Outgoing
   - ❑ Christian
   - ❑ Creative
   - ❑ Humble
   - ❑ Easygoing
   - ❑ Witty

   - ❑ Patient
   - ❑ Kind
   - ❑ Generous
   - ❑ Clean
   - ❑ Cheerful
   - ❑ Courageous
   - ❑ Responsible
   - ❑ Industrious

3. **Check out these Bible passages. What does each passage say about a friend?**
   Proverbs 17:17
   Proverbs 18:24
   Proverbs 27:6
   Proverbs 27:9-10

4. **Do you think each of these statements is T (true) or F (false)?**
   ___ A friend won't ever tell you what you don't want to hear.
   ___ A friend will stick with you no matter what.
   ___ A friend can be closer to you than a relative.
   ___ A friend will try to prevent another friend from making a bad choice.
   ___ Two friends will like the same things.
   ___ A friendship can be worn out by too much togetherness.
   ___ A Christian would be sure to tell their friends about Christ.
   ___ A Christian should only have Christian friends.

THERE FOR YOU [friendship—Proverbs 17, 18, 27]

THIS WEEK

Friendships are the heart and soul of the teenager years. As friendships increasingly important, junior highers and middle schoolers must learn what creates and sustains valuable and lasting friendships. They'll need to learn what kinds of friendships to build and to avoid—and what kind of friend they need to become. This TalkSheet will help the students to discover that friends can be one of the greatest gifts that God gives them.

OPENER

For this opener you'll need to give your students paper and pencils or pens. Tell them to draw seven columns on their paper with four rows across. In each column have them write the following headings—NAME, HOBBIES & INTERESTS, COLOR, PETS, ENTERTAINMENT, SPORTS, and WORST MOMENT. Then when you give the go, each kid must interview four other students and get all of the information from them—

• their first, middle, and last names
• any hobbies or interests (they must say something)
• their favorite colors
• what pets they have or have had
• their favorite movies, television programs, or bands
• any sports they enjoy
• and the worst moments in their lives.

You may want to give a small prize to the first person to get all seven columns completely filled. Then have a few willing students read out the information they discovered about others—they might be surprised what they learn. Then talk about how friendships often develop as people discover more about each other.

THE DISCUSSION, BY NUMBERS

1. You can use these questions to discuss the process of making and keeping friends. What is easy and difficult about these items? Discuss what might cause friendships to dissolve and what can make friendships last a long time. Why do people shift and change friendships? Is this a good thing or a bad thing?

2. Discuss the qualities of a real friend. Which qualities are the most important to have and why? What makes a friend a true friend? Do any of your kids have friends that have these qualities?

3. Ask for some of your students to share their answers (a friend loves at all times, loyalty is important, you can trust a real friend, you don't run out on your friends, and so on). You may want to make a list of the ideas from these verses. Why is a friend telling you bad news better than

flattery from an enemy? And why are friends important to have for advice and help?

4. What did your kids think of these items? Some of your kids may have both Christian and non-Christian friends. Talk about the pros and cons of having friends like them. How does this affect them at school or at church? You may want to talk about their opportunity and responsibility to share Christ with their unsaved friends.

THE CLOSE

Point out that it's just as important to be a friend as it is to make friends. Friendships take work, patience, and wisdom if they are going to last. Everyone is different. Some people are better at making friends than others and some people will have more friends than others. Some people are happy with a few close friends while others like to have lots of friends.

You may want to talk about some of the famous friendships in the Bible like David and Jonathan (see 1 Samuel 18 and 23), Jesus and his disciples (see Matthew, Mark, Luke, or John), and Paul and Timothy (see Acts, 1 Corinthians, or 1 and 2 Timothy). How are these examples of godly friendships? What characteristics of friendships were shown? How did these friends help each other and support each other?

MORE

● You may want to talk about friendship in the media—on TV, in movies, song lyrics, magazines, and so on. How do these portray friendship as opposed to what this proverb talks about? You may want to bring in (or have your kids bring in) articles, song lyrics, or clips of a TV show or movie. Talk about society's views of friendship versus God's views of friendship. How do these compare?

● Challenge each of your kids to encourage a friendship or two this week—to send a friend an e-mail or note, hang out with them, or something else. Maybe brainstorm some ways that your kids can work on their friendships. Then have them pay attention to how the friendship changed or grew from these efforts. Was it easy to work on the friendship? Why or why not? How did the other friend react?

TO TALK OR NOT TO TALK

1. You've just inherited a slew of money and now you want to invest it so that you'll have enough to buy a car, go to college, or buy a house. Circle **five** people from the list below who you'd most likely to go to for advice on what to do with your money.

Truck driver	Stockbroker	Close friend	Genius
Gambler	Bag lady	Banker	General
Real estate agent	Politician	Missionary	Teacher
Doctor	Five-year-old kid	Crook	Bankrupt person
IRS agent	Hitchhiker	Parent	Computer technician
Pastor	Accountant	Trash collector	Other—
Artist	Stranger on Web	Self-made millionaire	
Counterfeiter	chat room	Drunk	

2. Have you ever heard someone talk about something that—in reality— they knew little about it?

   If yes, what were your thoughts about the person while they were talking?

3. Check out **Proverbs 18:2**. In your own words, what do you think this proverb is talking about?

4. What subject or hobby do you know a lot about?

5. Your friend always has a lot to say about everything. The problem is, he doesn't really know a lot about most of the subjects or topics. Sometimes you're embarrassed for him because he makes such a fool of himself. You want to be his friend, but want to help him, too.

   What would you do in this situation?

   How do you think your friend would react if you confronted him?

TO TALK OR NOT TO TALK

[speaking wisely—Proverbs 18]

THIS WEEK

Everyone has an opinion. Some people—teenagers included—state their ideas on all kinds of things that they know nothing about. Godly wisdom, however, teaches people to seek understanding, insight, and knowledge. It teaches people to listen more than people talk. Just because people have the ability to express their opinions doesn't mean they always need to. This TalkSheet session will help your students see that while everyone has an opinion, not everyone is entitled to hold an opinion.

OPENER

Start off by asking your group to stand in the middle of the room. Tell all of the students who think foreign cars are better than domestic cars go to the left, and those who think domestic cars are better than foreign cars to the right. Then ask all those who think Ford builds better cars to go to the left side of the room, those who prefer Saturn to the middle, and those who consider Toyota to be the best to go to the right. Tell those who don't have a clue to sit down. You can try the same thing with different brands of cereal, clothing, and so on.

Point out that many of your kids have an opinion about most everything—and are quick to show it. With some things (like which breakfast is better) opinion really doesn't matter, but with other things (like cars) their opinion may show their ignorance or lack of knowledge on a topic.

THE DISCUSSION, BY NUMBERS

1. Your kids will mostly likely know who to go to for advice on money. You may want to make a list of their top five choices. Why would they go to these people? Discuss why people hold better opinions of some people than others.

2. Ask for a few volunteers to share their examples. Discuss what these people are doing to their reputation by talking about things they don't know about. How do they look to others? How does it make them feel?

3. What does this proverb say about friends? You may want to make a list of the friendship traits on a poster board or whiteboard. What makes a person a fool?

4. Which areas do your kids seem to have the most knowledge about? Talk about why a person can't be an expert in everything. How much does your group know about the Bible?

5. What would your kids say to someone who talks about what they don't know? Discuss ways to

respond when they're asked an opinion about something that they know little or nothing about. Why do some people act like they know a lot when they really don't?

THE CLOSE

Your kids often hear others giving an opinion on things they know little or nothing about. This is particularly true when it comes to the Bible. They'll hear ideas and opinions about the Bible from people who have never read it. Point out to your group that God wants people to speak wisely, to seek understanding and information rather than reacting blindly—he wants people to know what others are talking about. Challenge your kids to think about what they know before giving an opinion—and to challenge themselves to learn more about what they don't know.

MORE

● Ask your group members to research one topic on this week at home or at school—this doesn't have to be extensive. Just encourage them to find four or five new facts or pieces of information about a subject. Encourage them to search the Internet, ask an adult or teacher, or look in a book or magazine. Then have them bring their findings to share the info with the rest of the group. How did this knowledge help them? How easy or hard was it to find information? And was it worthwhile to learn about something new?

● Improve your kids' knowledge of the Bible and split them into small groups—then ask them to find a story in the Bible, read it as a group, and talk about what it means for Christians today. You may want to offer them suggestions of passages or stories. Then re-group and have the groups share what they read and learned. Point out that they can do this on their own—that's the best way to get closer with God and to understand him better.

OUT ON THE STREET

1. What do you think makes a person **poor**?

2. If you wanted to find a really poor person, where would you look?

3. If a person approached you on the street asking for money to buy food, what would you do?
   - ❏ Run
   - ❏ Ignore the person
   - ❏ Give the person money
   - ❏ Tell the person to get a job
   - ❏ Say you're broke and hungry, too
   - ❏ Buy some food for the person, but don't give any money
   - ❏ Give money if the person looked skinny and malnourished
   - ❏ Point the person to an shelter that feeds people

4. Check out **Proverbs 19:17** and Matthew **25:34-40**. According to these passages, what are you doing when you help the poor?

5. How do you think people would change if they knew that helping poor people was really helping God himself?

   How would your actions change?

OUT ON THE STREET [helping the poor—Proverbs 19]

THIS WEEK

Most people, including teenagers, live in an insulated world. They rarely starve and most have shelter. They seldom give a thought to those who—through no fault of their own—must scrape together even the basic necessities of life, like warmth and a simple meal.

This TalkSheet session is designed to heighten your students' awareness of the responsibility that Christians have to help those who suffer in poverty. The Bible gives a powerful message about God's identification with those in need. Kids will learn that to bless the poor is to bless God.

OPENER

Start out by asking each of your students to count the money in their pocket, purse, or wallet. Divide your group into the paupers (those who have no money at all), the poor (those with a dollar or less), the middle class (those with five dollars or less), and the rich (those with more than five dollars). Then, ask the paupers to sit on the floor in the back of the class or group. Next give the poor kids one chair to fight over and give the middle class one chair each. Finally, give all the extra chairs to the rich. You can do the same thing with any other items you might have, such as a box of cookies or sodas.

How does this activity make your group feel about the poor? What could the rich in the class have done with their abundance? What would happen if this were a real-life situation? How would your kids be living then?

THE DISCUSSION, BY NUMBERS

1. What do your kids think it means to be poor? Does it depend on what country they live in? What part of town? Make a list of their ideas on a poster board or whiteboard. Do any of your kids actually know a poor person? If so, how?

2. Your kids might not know anyone who is poor. Where might your kids find those who are poor? What causes some people to be poor? And are these people considered lazy sometimes? Why or why not?

3. What would your kids do in this situation? What is the easiest thing to do? How about the hardest? What is difficult about trying to decide if the need is real or a scam? Allow for some disagreement on this point.

4. These passages point out a surprising idea in the Bible—kindness to the poor is seen as kindness to God himself. Do your kids think Jesus was poor? Why or why not? You may want to point out

that he had no home, traveled and stayed with others, was fed by others, and hung out with those who were poor, too.

5. Ask the group to discuss how people might change if they seriously thought that it was God who they were taking care of or serving. What actions would your group like to take to help those in need?

THE CLOSE

How has your groups' perception and understanding of the poor changed? Point out that God has given people with a lot to share with those in need. How can your kids start to share what they have? Challenge your students to commit to participate in a program that would help those who are suffering from the effects of poverty. For more information check out World Vision (www.wvi.org) for information on their programs and resources for reaching out to those in need.

MORE

- Challenge your kids to participate in a 24-hour world hunger fast. You can do this as a group in a number of ways. Some groups gather pledges from people and use the fast as a fundraiser. Other groups simply start the fast with a prayer time, fast for 24 hours, and then debrief with a healthy meal at the end. Make sure you do this at a good time of the year when it's healthy for your kids to participate (you don't want parents calling to complain that their child can't play soccer because he hasn't eaten anything!) So, be sure to have parental support and involvement, too.
- Consider hosting a fundraiser or clothes drive for an agency in your area or for your church missionaries. Encourage your kids to collect clothes at their schools or host a theme or creative dinner at your church to raise money and collect clothes.

PEACEMAKER

1. Which of the following would irritate
you enough for you to fight about?
   - ❏ Someone cusses at you.
   - ❏ Someone cusses at your friend.
   - ❏ Someone accuses you of
     something you didn't do.
   - ❏ Someone shoves you around for
     no reason.
   - ❏ Someone tries to beat up
     your friend.
   - ❏ Someone tries to humiliate you in public.
   - ❏ Someone tries to hit on your girlfriend or boyfriend.
   - ❏ Someone tries to steal from you.

2. Put an X on the line to show your amount of patience or tolerance in an aggravating situation.

I'm extremely patient   Watch out if I'm mad

3. What do you think is the most brave thing to do—get into a fight or argument or control
yourself and walk away? Why?

4. Check out **Proverbs 20:3**. What would be the motto for each person, based on this verse?
The motto for a fool would be—

The motto for an honorable person would be—

5. How would you respond to these situations?
   a. You are threatened by a gang at school

   b. You are shoved by the school bully

   c. Your parents punish you unfairly

   d. Someone insults you

   e. Someone vandalizes your stuff

   f. You are cheated on by someone

PEACEMAKER [avoiding conflict—Proverbs 20]

THIS WEEK

Confrontations are a part of life. Unfortunately, society tells teenagers that violence is the best way to get back at others. In stark contrast, the Bible says that someone who avoids fighting is a person of honor. The bravest action in a confrontation is a peaceful one. This TalkSheet will help your students see that peacemakers truly are blessed.

OPENER

To start off this activity, write this phrase on a whiteboard or poster board—LITTLE WEAK GUY WIPES OUT BIG MEAN GUY. Now ask your students to think of books, movies, and TV shows where they've seen or read about a situation like this—where a so-called weaker character comes out on top. Make a master list of all the titles or characters and spend some time talking about how many of these movies, TV shows, and so on are based on truth and how many are based on fantasy. What normally happens when a little weak person goes against a big mean guy? How does Hollywood and the media portray confrontation among strong and weak characters? Based on what the media tells them, what does your group think a little weak person should do when confronted with a big mean person? How about women versus men? Teenagers versus adults? You may want to show a few clips of these movies before or afterward.

THE DISCUSSION, BY NUMBERS

1. What things most often draw your students into an argument or fight? Ask them to add any other situations that would anger them enough to want revenge. What causes people to fight? What problems do they think fighting or getting revenge solves?

2. How did your kids rate their tolerance or patience level? Ask for a few volunteers to share where they ranked themselves and why. How did the group rank as a whole—more toward patient or toward vengeful?

3. What is the more brave thing to do in a typical confrontation—fight or walk away? What do your students think about this? Can walking away from a confrontation make a person look cowardly? Why or why not? Let your kids disagree with each other if anything comes up. Would any of your kids think that fighting is the braver thing to do?

4. Make a list of the mottoes that your kids came up with. What are the differences between the two?

See if your students can reach a consensus on mottoes for an honorable person and for a fighting fool. Talk about the honor that comes with being a peacemaker. How much honor are your kids showing thorugh their actions?

5. How would your kids' mottos work in these situations? Make a list of their reactions. Talk about the kind of courage and self-control it takes to avoid a quarrel. In which situations (if any) would fighting be necessary?

THE CLOSE

Your kids might think this discussion is unrealistic. Some may have dealt with fighting and violence at home or school for years. Others may think the Bible is telling them to be a pushover or a wimp. Be sensitive to your group members who may find themselves in situations when they're forced to use self-defense. This proverb talks about avoiding foolish fighting and quarrels. How does this differ from defending against a physical attack or standing up for oneself in an argument? Pay attention to your kids who may be dealing with physical or sexual abuse, as well. Communicate clearly to the group that abuse of any kind is wrong. If any of your kids, or their friends, are dealing with abusive situations, they must find a trusted adult to talk with. Remind them that you are available to talk, too.

What practical ways can your kids apply this proverb to their lives? Point out that controlling anger takes self-control (see Livid or Let Go, pg. 81). God gives peace and self-control—if they ask him for it. Challenge your kids to keep this proverb in mind when dealing with confrontation and to remember that it's harder—but wiser—to avoid the fight.

MORE

● You may want to have your kids surf the Internet for information on hate groups—they are everywhere. Some include skinheads, neo-Nazis, and white supremacists. Discuss the motives behind these groups, what issues they're angry about, and what your kids can do to take stands for peace.

● Ask your students to each think of one person they typically have conflict with. Challenge your kids to pray for this person every day and put into practice peacekeeping actions and words. Be sure to follow up later and talk about any changes or progress made in these relationships during the following weeks. Did God use their prayers to help bring peace?

YOUR REPUTATION

1. Which of the following most closely describes your **reputation**?

   - ❏ Clown
   - ❏ Jock
   - ❏ Airhead
   - ❏ Studious
   - ❏ Spiritual
   - ❏ Outgoing
   - ❏ Computer nerd
   - ❏ Shy
   - ❏ Friendly

   - ❏ Humorous
   - ❏ Daring
   - ❏ Dumb
   - ❏ Smart
   - ❏ Tough
   - ❏ Hardworking
   - ❏ Mechanical
   - ❏ Pretty
   - ❏ Tasteful
   - ❏ Generous

   - ❏ Cool
   - ❏ Athletic
   - ❏ Moody
   - ❏ Clumsy
   - ❏ Brave
   - ❏ Old-fashioned
   - ❏ Progressive
   - ❏ Talented
   - ❏ Other—

2. Do you **agree** with this statement? Why or why not?
   A good reputation takes a long time to build, but only a moment to destroy.

3. Check out **Proverbs 22:1**. What does this verse mean to you?

4. Some things can help you have a good reputation, and some can bring a reputation down. Put a **plus sign (+)** next to the items that would give a person a good reputation, and a minus **sign (-)** next to the items you think would hurt your reputation.

   ___ Being a liar
   ___ Being patient
   ___ Being prejudiced
   ___ Being kind
   ___ Being funny
   ___ Being imaginative
   ___ Being generous
   ___ Being a gossip
   ___ Being devious

   ___ Being helpful
   ___ Being self-controlled
   ___ Being opinionated
   ___ Being quarrelsome
   ___ Being merciful
   ___ Being bossy
   ___ Being self-centered
   ___ Being cautious
   ___ Being caring

   ___ Being humble
   ___ Being proud
   ___ Being moral
   ___ Being immoral
   ___ Being boastful
   ___ Being loving
   ___ Being peaceful
   ___ Being hardworking
   ___ Being loyal

5. What do you think? Pick one of the questions below to answer in your own words.

   In what ways can a person **benefit** from having a good reputation?

   In what ways can a person **suffer** when she has a bad reputation?

   In what ways can a person **suffer** when he has a good reputation?

   In what ways can a person **benefit** when she has a bad reputation?

YOUR REPUTATION [reputation—Proverbs 22]

THIS WEEK

Teenagers want to be liked, admired, and accepted. They dress for the approval of their peers, act out roles for the applause of their peers, and are hurt when they are rejected. This TalkSheet session deals with a subject that is right where most students live every day—building a reputation that encourages others to like them. In this TalkSheet your group will learn that developing a good reputation takes effort and can be a struggle—but it's worth it!

OPENER

Start by bringing in some newspapers or magazines. Toss them on the floor and pass out a few pairs of scissors. Then ask your group to find and cut out advertisements that tie in the advertised product with a person's reputation (for example, what kind of reputation would a person equate with cigarettes?). What does the advertisement say about a person's reputation, appearance, or acceptance from others? Let your kids share their examples with each other and talk about why a reputation would be important to consumers. Why do people buy in to advertisements that promise to fix a person or improve a reputation? What other examples do your kids have? How affected do they think they are by the media and it's advertisements?

THE DISCUSSION, BY NUMBERS

1. What words would your kids pick to describe their reputation? If you don't want to ask for specific responses, ask the group if their reputation would be considered to be a negative? Why or why not? Take some time to talk about how reputations are created or built.

2. Discuss the process of building or destroying a reputation. What do kids do that ruins their reputation? You may want to have volunteer or two share a time when they hurt their reputation, what caused the problem, and what it took to repair their reputation.

3. What does the Bible say about a good reputation? Point out the value the Bible gives to a good name or reputation. How much would the price tag be if a person had to purchase a good reputation? You may want to ask the group to paraphrase this verse in their own words.

4. Explore the various characteristics or habits that can build or destroy a reputation. Note that the things that build a good reputation also fit with godly living. Which of these characteristics do your kids reflect in their lives? Which ones need some improvement?

5. Ask for some volunteers to share their ideas. You may want to make a list of their responses on a whiteboard or poster board. Point out the benefits of a good reputation—being trusted, being someone others come to for help and advice, gaining the respect of peers, and so on. What are the benefits of having a bad reputation, if any? Why do some kids with bad reputations become more popular than others?

THE CLOSE

A reputation is fragile. It can be shattered in a moment. Point out to the group that words and actions go hand in hand with one's character. Do the reputations of your kids reflect their characters? What kind of reputation are your kids after? Will this reputation hurt them in the end or not? Would they like to change their current reputation? You may want to discuss ways to repair a reputation and how to start over. Encourage them to start over with God and ask him for the strength to live for him.

MORE

● People who have certain reputations sometimes have nicknames. What nicknames have your kids heard for those with a certain reputation? Are these reputations and nicknames fair? Do they accurately reflect the person? Point out that nicknames are sometimes cruel ways of labeling people. Encourage your kids to look at others beyond the nicknames—and to reconsider the nicknames that they give to others.

● What are some other characteristics of a godly reputation? You may want to go through the Bible with your kids, or split them up into small groups, to look for examples and words that describe a Christ-like reputation and character. Point out that Jesus didn't have a good reputation among others because he helped those in need, hung out with sinners, and healed the weak. Sometimes it's not easy to have a godly reputation—God doesn't promise that it'll be easy. What characteristics do your kids need or want to work on? And are they willing to stand up to those who mock or challenge their beliefs?

GIMME, GIMME

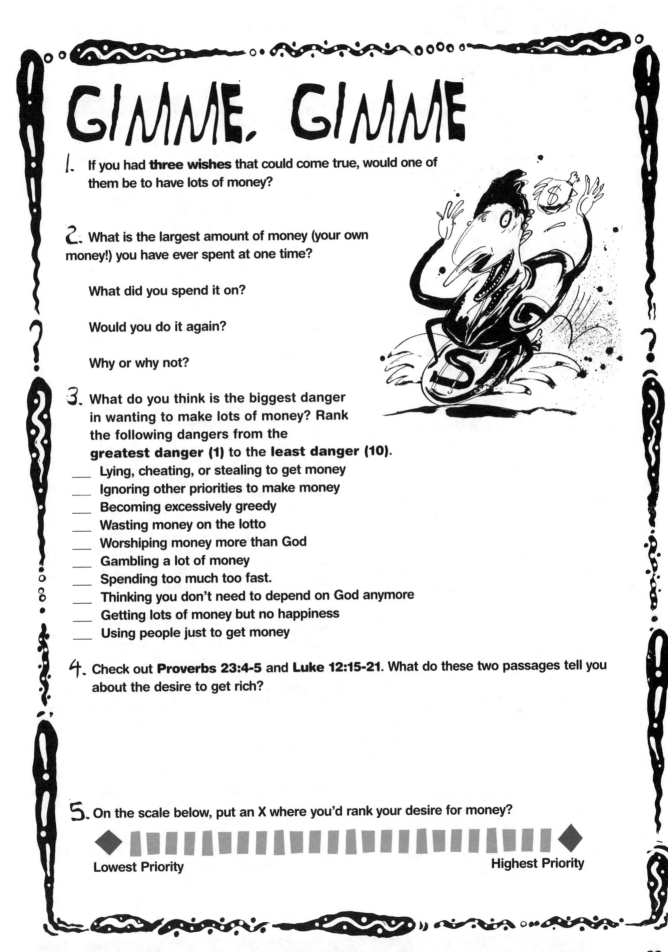

1. If you had **three wishes** that could come true, would one of them be to have lots of money?

2. What is the largest amount of money (your own money!) you have ever spent at one time?

   What did you spend it on?

   Would you do it again?

   Why or why not?

3. What do you think is the biggest danger in wanting to make lots of money? Rank the following dangers from the **greatest danger (1)** to the **least danger (10)**.

   ___ Lying, cheating, or stealing to get money
   ___ Ignoring other priorities to make money
   ___ Becoming excessively greedy
   ___ Wasting money on the lotto
   ___ Worshiping money more than God
   ___ Gambling a lot of money
   ___ Spending too much too fast.
   ___ Thinking you don't need to depend on God anymore
   ___ Getting lots of money but no happiness
   ___ Using people just to get money

4. Check out **Proverbs 23:4-5** and **Luke 12:15-21**. What do these two passages tell you about the desire to get rich?

5. On the scale below, put an X where you'd rank your desire for money?

   Lowest Priority ◆▮▮▮▮▮▮▮▮▮▮▮▮▮▮▮▮▮◆ **Highest Priority**

GIMME, GIMME [greed—Proverbs 23]

THIS WEEK

Most junior highers and middle schoolers don't have thousands in the bank—but they know about the power of money. Society has taught them that happiness and money are directly related. The Bible gives people a different perspective on wealth. It warns kids and adults that the minute they fix their gaze on the dollar, it sprouts wings and flies away. This TalkSheet session is designed to help your students to understand that eternal treasures aren't made of money.

OPENER

Tell your students that they must choose a career. One job pays $100,000 per year but is really stressful and difficult. The other job is really fun, but pays barely enough to get by. Ask your students to select the job they would choose for a career, and to go to the side of the room that reflects their choice—side one with great pay or side two with enjoyable work. After they've chosen their sides, discuss the reasons for their choices. Make a list of their ideas and priorities for choosing what they did. Have their parents had to deal with these situations? What do they think most people in the world do in this situation? How about missionaries, pastors, or private-school teachers? Use this discussion as an opportunity to introduce today's topic.

Or you may want to bring in a stack of ads from the Sunday paper, some magazines with advertisements, or some catalogs, etc. Break the your group into clusters of three to five and ask them to cut out stuff from the ads that they personally own and stuff that they want to have. Then have them make two stacks of the cut out ads—things they have and things they want to have. Ask the groups to compare which stack is bigger. Do they need the stuff they want? Why or why not?

THE DISCUSSION, BY NUMBERS

1. Would your kids want to have money? Take a poll of the groups' responses and use this question to further the discussion of their desire for money. Why does money appear on so many of their wish lists? What would they rather have, their health or lots of money?

2. How did your kids spend their money? What did they buy? Check out if any of them had regrets about the money they've spent. Point out that sometimes people burn with desire for some object, but become bored with it once they've gotten it. Have your kids experienced this in their own lives?

3. How did your kids rank these items? Rank them as a group and decide which one is the most dangerous and why. What problems does money make in your kids' spiritual lives? Which difficulties seem most dangerous to your students?

4. What do these verses say about wealth? How do these verses apply to your kids' lives? You may want to have them rewrite these verses in their own words and to insert their own examples. Then have a few of them share what they wrote.

5. How important is making money to your kids? If you don't want to ask for specific responses, ask how many of them rank more toward the right or left. Where would teenagers in general put themselves on this scale? Where on this scale should a warning flag go? What can your kids do to keep a godly perspective on money?

THE CLOSE

Society is consumed with material things and living the good life. Some of your kids may have parents, family members, or friends who have a lot of money—and spend it. Point out the danger of getting caught up in the "gimme" mentality. It's hard not to get caught up in spending money in a society focused on advertisements and shopping malls. Encourage your students to make a priority of investing in things that can't be taken away—their faith in God, their relationships with others, and who they are as a person. Challenge them to bring their needs and desires to God and to trust him with their wants.

MORE

● How do advertisements affect materialism and consumerism? Ask your kids to make a list of everywhere they see advertisements—on clothing, on buses, on the Internet, and even on cereal boxes. Where do they see advertising? How does advertising influence people to buy things they don't need? How can your kids keep advertisements from getting to them? You may want to show a few videotaped commercials and talk about the message that is given.

● How do your kids spend their money—or the allowance that their parents give them? Ask your kids to keep track of everything that they spend money on in a given week and write it down. Then talk with them about what they bought and whether or not the item(s) was something they needed or wanted. They'll be surprised to see how they've spent their money!

BE A LIFESAVER

1. Who would you most likely **risk your life** to save?

   baby   sibling
   old person   pet
   criminal   friend
   parent   stranger

2. Do you think this statement is **true** or **false**? Why or why not?
   People who need spiritual help should be given urgent attention, like people who need physical help.

3. Check out **Proverbs 24:11-12** and answer the following questions.

   Who is this passage directed to?

   Who is it talking about?

   What is their problem?

   What should people do about it?

   How might people try to avoid their responsibility?

   How could their actions be judged?

4. How might a person be led to **spiritual death**?

5. Suppose you wanted rescue some friends from dying spiritually. List—in order of effectiveness—which ways would be the best to conduct the rescue, with **1 being the most effective.**

   ___ E-mail them some info about Christ   ___ Preach a sermon to them
   ___ Bring them to a church service   ___ Tell them what Christ means to you
   ___ Give them a Bible   ___ Pray for them
   ___ Send the pastor over to talk to them   ___ Loan them a Christian CD
   ___ Act all spiritual around them   ___ Bring them to youth group
   ___ Give them a gospel booklet or tract   ___ Wear a Christian tee shirt

6. What are some **excuses** that teenagers come up with for not trying to rescue their friends from a spiritual death?

BE A LIFESAVER [sharing Christ—Proverbs 24]

THIS WEEK

The Great Commission is clearly stated—to tell others the good news of Jesus Christ, regardless of age. Young teens rub shoulders daily with those who are being led away to spiritual death by false ideas from a secular world. Christians are called to the rescue—but the responsibility to share Christ with friends is scary to teenagers. This TalkSheet session is designed to let students know that there is an effective and easy way to share what Jesus Christ means to them personally, in their own words and their own ways.

OPENER

Present this scenario (or one like it) to your kids—your family has decided to host a foreign exchange student from India for the coming school year. This person is an excellent student, which has qualified him or her to study in the United States. Upon his or her arrival, you discover that he or she is a devout Hindu. After months of hanging out with you, your friends, and your family, he or she asks you to explain your religion and why you love this God person so much. What would your kids say to this person? How would they share their Christian faith with these beings who have never heard one word about Jesus Christ before? What would be the hardest or easiest part about sharing their faith? How does this compare with sharing your faith with friends at school or others that you meet? Which situation would be easier? Why or why not?

THE DISCUSSION, BY NUMBERS

1. Who would your kids be the most likely risk their lives for? Take a poll of the group and ask for some volunteers to share the reasons for their answers. Point out that most people would risk a lot to save one of their friends. Why?

2. How did your kids answer this question? How are spiritual needs as important as physical needs? Help your group define what spiritual needs are—that students' very souls are in jeopardy without God.

3. Be prepared for some strong reactions to this passage. It will be hard for some to face their responsibilities. Some may have a hard time facing up to the reality of hell. Spend some time talking about this. But don't use hell as a threat—a relationship with God is more than that, it's a personal friendship with someone who loves them.

4. Help your group understand how the everyday, unhealthy activities that any of people can fall into—obsession with money, sexual temptation, and so on—can actually lead to a slow spiritual death. How do these sins pull people further away from God?

5. Discuss which method of telling others about Christ is the most effective. Let your young people brainstorm on this and ask your students what would have the most effect on them. Point out that everyone is different—some people feel more comfortable sharing than others. Help them to find a way that works for them.

6. What are some excuses teenagers give? You may want to make a list of the excuses on a poster board or whiteboard. What's the most common excuse? Point out that they don't have to be theological experts—they just have to share what God has done for them, in their own words.

THE CLOSE

Close by reading Ephesians 2:1-5 and point out that spiritual death is the result of not knowing Christ personally. Some of your kids may be on a journey toward spiritual death. You may want to present the message of salvation to your kids and the group some time to pray either with the group or on their own. Be careful not to pressure or scare your kids into making a commitment that they might not be ready for. Some of them may have a lot more answers about salvation and Christ. Communicate that you're available to talk and answer questions. Finally, challenge them to ask God for the strength and words to share with others. God speaks through his spirit. He'll give them the words if they let God use them for sharing his love to others.

MORE

● You may want to do some kind of reach-out with your kids during the next week or so. Challenge your group members to think of at least one person that they will attempt to share Christ with in some way—and to follow up on that. Brainstorm with your group how they can be a witness to others and then do it. Keep track of what has happened since this discussion and talk about any challenges that they may have faced.

● Give your group the tools that they need to share the gospel—the essential verses they can use as ammo when presenting the love of God to others. Spend some time reading these verses with your group and ask them to put the verses in their own words. Check out the Romans Road to Salvation—Romans 3:10, Romans 3:23, Romans 5:12, Romans 6:23, Romans 5:8-9, and Romans 10:9-13—or print it out for your group at http://hmiministries.org/romans.htm or http://www.pfbaptistpress.org/29.htm.

EVEN MY ENEMY?

1. Who is someone that you would consider an enemy? Put that person's initials here—

2. Put an arrow by the top **three ways** that you think people typically handle their enemies.

   Put them down whenever possible.
   Help them out if they are in need.
   Physically hurt the person.
   Think about ways to hurt them.
   Cuss the person out.
   Talk to them on the phone.
   Try to get them into trouble.
   Threaten their friends.
   Sabotage their locker.

   Send them anonymous, harsh e-mails.
   Pull a gun on them.
   Spread rumors about the person.
   Dislike their friends and family, too.
   Look for ways to bless them.
   Talk to them kindly.
   Ignore the person.
   Pray for them.
   Hope they die a slow and painful death.

3. Check out **Proverbs 25:21-22**; **Matthew 5:43-48**; and **Romans 12:14**. What specific instructions do these passages give for how to treat an enemy?

4. Write down **three things** that your enemies might do or say if you treated them like Christ commanded.

5. If treating their enemies the way Jesus commanded is the goal for Christians, how successful are you in reaching that goal? Mark your position on the line below.

 ▮▮▮▮▮▮▮▮▮▮▮▮▮▮▮▮▮▮▮▮▮▮▮▮

Failing miserably

Always like Jesus

EVEN MY ENEMY? [loving your enemies— Proverbs 25]

THIS WEEK

Through movies, TV shows, and violence in society, junior highers and middle schoolers have learned to deal with enemies in a manner far different than that required by Jesus. Christ's teaching is radically different from what your kids may think—in fact, they may pull back in surprise at this session. Your kids may struggle with the plan God lays out for dealing with enemies and maybe can't imagine how it would help them. This TalkSheet session provides a great opportunity to challenge students to see if they really trust God enough to follow his commands.

OPENER

Draw up a list of 20 feuding or competing pairs that your kids would know, both real and fictional such as—
- **The Road Runner and Wile E. Coyote**
- **Microsoft and Apple**
- **Darth Vader and Luke Skywalker**
- **Coke and Pepsi**
- **McDonalds and Burger King**
- **NBC and ABC**

(Use your brains to come up with some more your kids will know!) Then use this list to hold a fun contest with your kids.

Pass out pieces of paper to each of your kids with one-half of the adversary pairs listed. Their task is to find the second half of the correct adversary. Or if you're group isn't big enough for that, have your kids write down who they think the other adversary is. You may want to give small prizes to those who get the most correct pairs.

THE DISCUSSION, BY NUMBERS

1. As you discuss your kids' enemies, be sure not to ask for names. Instead, ask them how the person became their enemy. What did the person say or do to them? How have your kids responded to their enemies—in good or bad ways?

2. How do people typically handle their enemies? How do people usually treat those who they think of as enemies? You may want to ask which of the ways listed seem crazy and why. How does society in general treat their enemies?

3. What does the Bible say about dealing with an enemy? You may want to make a list of their ideas on a poster board or whiteboard. Discuss how this conflicts with the way people usually treat those they dislike. Do your kids think it'd be easy to follow these commands? Why or why not?

4. How would your kids' enemies respond if they were treated as Christ instructed? Have a few willing students share their answers. Then ask them this—how would you react if your enemy treated you as Christ commanded?

5. Where do your kids rank on this scale? If you don't want to ask for specific rankings, ask how many of them rank more toward the right (or left). Why is loving your enemies hard for most people to do? Challenge your kids to start treating their enemies as Christ commanded. Where would your kids like to rank themselves in a few months? A year? Five years?

THE CLOSE

Explain to your group that it's difficult—but not impossible—to treat enemies with love and kindness. Point out that this process is done one step at a time, starting with something simple such as refusing to get back at a person or spread gossip. Encourage your group members to ask God for help in dealing with their enemies and to ask him for the strength to love the enemy back. Challenge them to pray for one enemy during the week and to see what happens—does the relationship improve? Why or why not? What is God teaching them about love, patience, and perseverance?

MORE

- Ask your students to rewrite Matthew 5:43-48 by substituting the name of a person who they would consider their enemy for the word enemy. What does this verse say to them? Is this verse an encouragement to them or not? How do these verses relate with being a Christian?
- How did some biblical characters handle their enemies? You may want to take a look at some of these stories and examples. Check out the relationship between Jesus and Satan (Matthew 4:1-10), Jacob and Esau (Genesis 27:41), Esther and Mordecai (Esther 9), David and Goliath (1 Samuel 17:1-54), or Joseph and his brothers (Genesis 37). How did God work in these relationships and what happened? Note how God used the bad for the good—the same thing he can do with enemies today.

YOU'RE ALL THAT!

1. Which of the following people interest you and which turn you off? Mark an **I for interest** and a **T for turn off**—or if you're neutral, leave the space blank.

   ___ A quiet person
   ___ Someone who compares themselves to others
   ___ Someone who constantly talks about others
   ___ Someone who lets you in on secrets
   ___ Someone who asks you about yourself
   ___ A humorous or funny person
   ___ Someone who brags about their exploits and daring deeds
   ___ Someone who has ideas that are new to you

2. Why do you think people react **negatively** toward those who brag about themselves?

3. Check out **Proverbs 27:2** and summarize this verse in your own words.

4. Do you feel good when someone compliments you? Why or why not?

5. Who is someone that you know and like? Make a list of some praiseworthy things about this person in the space below.

6. Which **three ideas** below do you think are the best ways to get complimented by others?
   ❏ Go around fishing for compliments
   ❏ Thank people profusely when they say something nice
   ❏ Ask for other peoples' ideas
   ❏ Flatter or kiss up to other people
   ❏ Say something when someone does a good thing
   ❏ Do something sacrificial
   ❏ Build yourself up
   ❏ Be a loyal friend
   ❏ Look for the good in others
   ❏ Have a cheerful attitude

YOU'RE ALL THAT! [becoming praiseworthy—Proverbs 27]

THIS WEEK

Everyone likes to hear good things about themselves. People like to know that they're valuable to other people. Young teens especially need acceptance and welcome from their peers. This TalkSheet session focuses on the foolishness of declaring their own importance and on ways that students can become the kind of people that others will want to praise— primarily by making other people feel important.

OPENER

Start off by telling your group the Greek fable of Echo and Narcissus.

There once was a nymph of the forest named Echo. She was cursed by the goddess Hera and could only speak the last words she heard others say. One day Echo spied a golden-haired man hunting deer in the woods. His name was Narcissus, and he was the most handsome young man in the forest—and the most conceited.

When Echo saw Narcissus, she immediately fell in love with him. She stepped from behind the tree and rushed to embrace Narcissus.

But he pushed her away and shouted, "Leave me alone! I'd rather die than let you love me!"

Humiliated and filled with sorrow, Echo wandered the mountains until she found a cave to live in alone. Meanwhile Narcissus hunted in the woods, until one day he discovered a hidden pool of water. Tired from hunting and eager to quench his thirst, Narcissus lay on his stomach and leaned over the water. But when he looked at the glassy surface, he saw someone staring back at him. Narcissus was spellbound. But when he leaned down and tried to kiss the perfect lips, he kissed only spring water. When he reached out and tried to embrace this vision of beauty, it disappeared in the water.

Day after day, Narcissus stared at the water, in love with his own reflection. He began to waste away from grief, until one sad morning, he felt himself dying. "Good-bye, my love!" he shouted to his reflection and then he died.

After sharing the story, point out that that some people seem to be in love with themselves—they're selfish, conceited, or prideful. What examples of self-aborption and conceit have they seen in people at school, family members, and so on?

THE DISCUSSION, BY NUMBERS

1. What interests or turns off your kids? Take a poll of your group and see what actions are the most offensive. Why do your kids think some people brag? And does the bragger know that he's probably offending others?

2. What makes bragging a negative thing? Ask for a few volunteers to share their responses. Ask your kids What makes people feel uncomfortable around those who brag?

3. What does this verse mean to your kids? Why is this good wisdom to follow? Ask for a few to summarize the verse in their owns words.

4. How does it feel to be complimented and appreciated? You may want to make a list of the group's ideas. Discuss what people like about genuine praise.

5. Make a list of all the praiseworthy qualities about a person that they like and admire. Have your kids ever indicated to their friend what they appreciate about them? Discuss how people might feel if they knew how praiseworthy and appreciated they were.

6. What's the best way to get complimented? Talk about what makes a person important and praiseworthy to others. Point out what is most likely to create genuine appreciation—being someone who genuinely appreciates others!

THE CLOSE

Let your students know that God's idea of being important to others involves making others feel important. Point out that the quickest way to be alienated from others is to brag about your own worthiness and importance. Challenge your students to look for opportunities to praise their friends and family members.

MORE

● Who in your church is contributing a lot of effort and energy? Your pastor? Missionaries? Janitor? Others? Brainstorm with your group and consider doing something encouraging for that person as an appreciation, such as a huge thank-you card or a special gift. Encourage your kids to do the same with their friends or family members during the week.

● Or try the hot seat of encouragement with your group. Have your group sit in a circle on chairs or on the floor. Put a chair in the middle of the circle. Then take have your kids take turns sitting in the seat in the middle. Ask the rest of the group to think of things that they would be thankful for if they were the person in the seat. Encourage them to include compliments and encouraging remarks and comments. If you don't want to play this way, have your group pick names and write down their thoughts, then return the list to the person who they picked.

COMING CLEAN

1. Do you think it's **easy** or **hard** to cover up something wrong that you've done? Why?

2. What are the **top five reasons** people cover up the things they do wrong?
   - ❑ They're afraid that others will think they are weird.
   - ❑ They're ashamed of what they did.
   - ❑ They're afraid of what their parents will say.
   - ❑ They think others will see them as hypocrites.
   - ❑ They're afraid of punishment.
   - ❑ They don't want to be humiliated in public.
   - ❑ They're afraid they will get a police record.
   - ❑ They're afraid they will get a bad reputation.
   - ❑ They'll have to stop doing what they are doing.
   - ❑ They think it's more fun if no one knows about it.

3. Alex was caught shoplifting. As part of his punishment, his parents made him go to the manager and each person who worked in the store and apologize to each one of them.
   Do you think the punishment was—
   - ❑ Fair and just
   - ❑ A sure way to cure shoplifting
   - ❑ Too harsh
   - ❑ Child abuse
   - ❑ Too embarrassing
   - ❑ Stupid and ineffective

4. Check out **Proverbs 28:13, Isaiah 29:15,** and **1 John 1:8-9**. What do these verses say about hiding your sins?

5. Should people ever confess their wrongdoings to someone else? Why or why not?

   If yes, who should people confess to?

   If you wanted to confess your wrongdoing, who would you go to now?

COMING CLEAN

THIS WEEK

Kids—like most human beings—find it hard to confess when they've done wrong. Sins can stay to haunt and make people feel guilty. That's one reason that the Bible urges confession. It's a healthy cleansing process—the beginning of mercy and forgiveness. There's no reality check like admitting their failures. This TalkSheet session will encourage your students to be honest about their spiritual failures. Your kids will be challenged to quickly admit their sins to God.

OPENER

You may want to use this illustration (or one like it) to start things off. Before your meeting, fill a backpack with some large rocks. On each rock, write a sin (either on the rock or a piece of tape on the rock)—examples include lying, cheating, stealing, swearing, etc. Zip up the backpack or bag. During your intro, ask for some volunteers to come up to the front of the room. Have them put the backpack on and describe how it feels to have the pack on. Make a master list of the words that they use to describe the weight or how it feel to have the pack on. Then open up the backpack and pull out the stones. Point out that each stone has something written on it—a sin that needs confessing. Point out that just like the backpack, unconfessed sin wears people down—it's a burden that they carry around. Use this activity to jumpstart your discussion on confessing sins, getting forgiveness, and letting God carry the load.

THE DISCUSSION, BY NUMBERS

1. Is it easier or harder for your kids to hide or to conceal wrongdoing. Why? What does God think about confessions sins? How can this bring you closer to God?

2. What are the top five reasons why people try to cover up wrongdoing? What do your kids think is the worst way to try to cover something up? Why? You may want to ask for some volunteers to tell about a time when they covered up a wrongdoing and what happened.

3. Take a poll of your kids' answers. How effective do they think his punishment was? Ask if Alex's confession was valid, since it was forced. Will it keep him from stealing again? Does your group think Alex learned his lesson? Why or why not?

4. These verses discuss confession of sin and the uselessness of concealment. You may want to read the verses with the group and ask for volunteers to fill in the blanks on a whiteboard or poster board.

Point out that God is all-knowing—he knows when people mess up and sin. But he also wants to forgive and have mercy.

5. Talk about when and if people should confess their sins to another person and even ask for forgiveness. Who would your kids go to and why? How many of them would go to God first? If your kids want to talk with someone, what qualities do they look for in a confidant?

THE CLOSE

Following up from the intro, point out that God's taken sin—like the rocks—and thrown them into the deepest part of the sea. When people confess, their sins are gone. God lovingly offers forgiveness and mercy to those who learn the habit of confessing. And he's waiting for your kids to bring their distresses, concerns, and wrong doings to him. He knows about them anyway—and he's willing to listen. Encourage your kids to ask God for forgiveness—and if they need someone else to talk with, to find an adult (let them know that you're available, too). God forgives and forgets. Period. What's holding your kids back today?

MORE

● You may want to talk more about how holding sin in can affect trust and respect in relationships. How can unconfessed sin hurt a friendship, a relationship with a boyfriend or girlfriend, or relationships with parents? What happens when someone is caught in a sin? What happens when someone hurts someone else and doesn't ask that person for forgiveness? Challenge your kids to get right with the people that they've hurt and to get the burden of that sin off their back.

● To help your kids to appreciate the benefits of honesty, try this activity—note that you may want a high level of trust within your group. Remind your kids of the TalkSheet ground rule about confidentiality and group trust. Then ask your kids to share one sin or cover-up of a sin (or lie) that they wish they could erase and why. Maybe jumpstart this activity by telling them one of yours.

WORDS TO LIVE BY

1. Do you think each statement is **T (true)** or
   F (false)?
   ___ The Bible could be God's Word.
   ___ The Bible is an old book of myths and fables.
   ___ The Bible has some of God's words in it.
   ___ The Bible is God's Word.

2. What do you think? Pick one response to complete the sentence.
   When people read the Bible, they should—
   ❏ believe and follow only what their heart tells them to
   ❏ believe and follow only what their church or pastor tells them to
   ❏ study carefully, then obey what is clearly taught
   ❏ see its contents as suggestions rather than strict guidelines
   ❏ enjoy it as literature

3. Many religions have their own holy books. Some groups have added to or taken away
   from what's found in the Bible. What would you say to someone if they insisted that they
   had a new and improved version of God's Word?

4. Check out the following verses and match each one with what it teaches.
   Proverbs 30:5   God's Word is flawless.
   Luke 11:28   The Word of God is like a sword that cuts to your heart.
   2 Timothy 3:15-16   God told the writers what to write.
   Hebrews 4:12   Those who hear and obey God's Word are blessed.

5. Why do you think some Christians spend little time reading Bible?

6. Which is true for you?
   ❏ I read the Bible a lot.
   ❏ I need to read the Bible more.
   ❏ I am comfortable with how much I read the Bible.
   ❏ I read the Bible, but I don't obey much of what it says.

From *Junior High-Middle School TalkSheets Psalms and Proverbs—Updated!* by Rick Bundschuh and Tom Finley. Permission to reproduce this page granted only for use in the buyer's own youth group. www.YouthSpecialties.com

109

WORDS TO LIVE BY [the Bible—Proverbs 30]

THIS WEEK

The writer of Proverbs tells people that every word of God is flawless. Human wisdom can't even come close to the incredible illumination that comes from God's word. Are your kids bored with the Bible? Do they find it dull and inapplicable to their lives? Through this TalkSheet, your kids will discover that God provides people a refuge, a rule of instruction for living life, a love letter, and an instrument for touching the most private aspects of their lives—all packaged in pages of paper and ink.

OPENER

Bring in an instruction book for any device—from a computer, TV, microwave, radio, DVD player, or more. Ask your group how many of them (or their parents) actually read instruction books. How many tend to avoid them or only read them when they are stuck? Talk about how people can mess up their purchases when people fail to follow the instruction manuals. Compare this with the Bible—God's instruction manual for human beings. How do people mess up their lives by not following his word?

THE DISCUSSION, BY NUMBERS

1. Take a poll of your group members to see how they responded. Discuss the various viewpoints on the authority of the Bible. Where have your kids learned about the Bible?

2. Ask for a few volunteers to share their responses. What does your group think? How should a person respond to the Bible, if they love and honor God?

3. How could your kids respond in this situation? Point out that the Bible has survived innumerable attacks, alterations, and other abuses—and still powerfully testifies to a risen Christ. Is it hard to defend the truth and authority of the Bible? Why or why not?

4. What does the Bible says about itself? You may want to read each verse with the group and discuss them. How does this information relate to the previous questions?

5. Why do your kids think this happens? Maybe because some fear that it's hard to understand, fear of seeing challenging commands from God, and so on. Have a few willing students share why they may have trouble spending time in the Bible, and share your struggles (if you have any) with regular Bible reading.

6. Ask your students to evaluate how seriously they take the Bible to be God's Word. Talk about ways to make the Bible easier to access for them—topical Bible discussions, devotional guides, and the like.

THE CLOSE

Point out that it's important to spend time reading about God and his word in the Bible. You may want to brainstorm and format at least one devotional plan that your kids could implement during the week. What realistic, tangible goal will they set for themselves? How much are they willing to commit to spending time with God? And can they come through on their commitment?

Brainstorm ways that your kids can get into the Bible. Recommend student versions of Bibles including the Teen Devotional Bible (Youth Specialties) or the New Student Bible (Zondervan). Encourage them to find a version of the Bible that works for them. If a typical NIV is too hard for them to understand, have them find a version that is easier to read. You may also want to suggest some study tools or have them check out some student Web sites (such as www.christianteens.net or www.teens4god.com) where your kids can download devotions, find information, and learn more about how to grow in their faith.

MORE

● You may want to consider doing an in-group Bible study with your group, or part of your group. There are a lot of tangible Bible resources out there for junior highers and middle schoolers, including the Wild Truth series. For more information on these resources, check out www.YouthSpecialties.com.

● There are quite a few stimulating, challenging Bible trivia games available. These are great ways to teach your kids while learning new stuff, too. Play one of these games with your kids or create a Bible trivia game with your group. Have them write their own questions based on the Bible. The game can be played at your next meeting or retreat. You can find helpful Bible trivia questions at www.Biblequizzes.com or www.bible-trivia.com.

RESOURCES FROM YOUTH SPECIALTIES

YOUTH MINISTRY PROGRAMMING

Camps, Retreats, Missions, & Service Ideas (Ideas Library)
Compassionate Kids: Practical Ways to Involve Your Students in Mission and Service
Creative Bible Lessons from the Old Testament
Creative Bible Lessons in 1 & 2 Corinthians
Creative Bible Lessons in John: Encounters with Jesus
Creative Bible Lessons in Romans: Faith on Fire!
Creative Bible Lessons on the Life of Christ
Creative Bible Lessons in Psalms
Creative Junior High Programs from A to Z, Vol. 1 (A-M)
Creative Junior High Programs from A to Z, Vol. 2 (N-Z)
Creative Meetings, Bible Lessons, & Worship Ideas (Ideas Library)
Crowd Breakers & Mixers (Ideas Library)
Downloading the Bible Leader's Guide
Drama, Skits, & Sketches (Ideas Library)
Drama, Skits, & Sketches 2 (Ideas Library)
Dramatic Pauses
Everyday Object Lessons
Games (Ideas Library)
Games 2 (Ideas Library)
Games 3 (Ideas Library)
Good Sex: A Whole-Person Approach to Teenage Sexuality and God
Great Fundraising Ideas for Youth Groups
More Great Fundraising Ideas for Youth Groups
Great Retreats for Youth Groups
Holiday Ideas (Ideas Library)
Hot Illustrations for Youth Talks
More Hot Illustrations for Youth Talks
Still More Hot Illustrations for Youth Talks
Ideas Library on CD-ROM
Incredible Questionnaires for Youth Ministry
Junior High Game Nights
More Junior High Game Nights
Kickstarters: 101 Ingenious Intros to Just about Any Bible Lesson
Live the Life! Student Evangelism Training Kit
Memory Makers
The Next Level Leader's Guide
Play It! Over 150 Great Games for Youth Groups
Roaring Lambs
Special Events (Ideas Library)
Spontaneous Melodramas
Spontaneous Melodramas 2
Student Leadership Training Manual
Student Underground: An Event Curriculum on the Persecuted Church
Super Sketches for Youth Ministry
Talking the Walk
Teaching the Bible Creatively
Videos That Teach
What Would Jesus Do? Youth Leader's Kit
Wild Truth Bible Lessons
Wild Truth Bible Lessons 2
Wild Truth Bible Lessons—Pictures of God
Wild Truth Bible Lessons—Pictures of God 2
Worship Services for Youth Groups

PROFESSIONAL RESOURCES

Administration, Publicity, & Fundraising (Ideas Library)
Dynamic Communicators Workshop
Equipped to Serve: Volunteer Youth Worker Training Course
Help! I'm a Junior High Youth Worker!
Help! I'm a Small-Group Leader!
Help! I'm a Sunday School Teacher!
Help! I'm a Volunteer Youth Worker!
How to Expand Your Youth Ministry
How to Speak to Youth...and Keep Them Awake at the Same Time
Junior High Ministry (Updated & Expanded)
The Ministry of Nurture: A Youth Worker's Guide to Discipling Teenagers
Postmodern Youth Ministry
Purpose-Driven® Youth Ministry
Purpose-Driven® Youth Ministry Training Kit
So That's Why I Keep Doing This! 52 Devotional Stories for Youth Workers
A Youth Ministry Crash Course
Youth Ministry Management Tools
The Youth Worker's Handbook to Family Ministry

ACADEMIC RESOURCES

Four Views of Youth Ministry & the Church
Starting Right: Thinking Theologically About Youth Ministry

DISCUSSION STARTERS

Discussion & Lesson Starters (Ideas Library)
Discussion & Lesson Starters 2 (Ideas Library)
EdgeTV
Get 'Em Talking
Keep 'Em Talking!
Good Sex: A Whole-Person Approach to Teenage Sexuality & God
High School TalkSheets—Updated!
More High School TalkSheets—Updated!
High School TalkSheets Psalms and Proverbs—Updated!
Junior High and Middle School TalkSheets—Updated!
More Junior High and Middle School TalkSheets—Updated!
Junior High and Middle School TalkSheets Psalms and Proverbs—Updated!
Real Kids: Short Cuts
Real Kids: The Real Deal—on Friendship, Loneliness, Racism, & Suicide
Real Kids: The Real Deal—on Sexual Choices, Family Matters, & Loss
Real Kids: The Real Deal—on Stressing Out, Addictive Behavior, Great Comebacks, & Violence
Real Kids: Word on the Street
Unfinished Sentences: 450 Tantalizing Statement-Starters to Get Teenagers Talking & Thinking
What If...? 450 Thought-Provoking Questions to Get Teenagers Talking, Laughing, and Thinking
Would You Rather...? 465 Provocative Questions to Get Teenagers Talking
Have You Ever...? 450 Intriguing Questions Guaranteed to Get Teenagers Talking

ART SOURCE CLIP ART

Stark Raving Clip Art (print)
Youth Group Activities (print)
Clip Art Library Version 2.0 CD-ROM

DIGITAL RESOURCES

Clip Art Library Version 2.0 CD-RPOM
Ideas Library on CD-ROM
Youth Ministry Management Tools

VIDEOS AND VIDEO CURRICULUMS

Dynamic Communicators Workshop
EdgeTV
Equipped to Serve: Volunteer Youth Worker Training Course
The Heart of Youth Ministry: A Morning with Mike Yaconelli
Live the Life! Student Evangelism Training Kit
Purpose-Driven® Youth Ministry Training Kit
Real Kids: Short Cuts
Real Kids: The Real Deal—on Friendship, Loneliness, Racism, & Suicide
Real Kids: The Real Deal—on Sexual Choices, Family Matters, & Loss
Real Kids: The Real Deal—on Stressing Out, Addictive Behavior, Great Comebacks, & Violence
Real Kids: Word on the Street
Student Underground: An Event Curriculum on the Persecuted Church
Understanding Your Teenager Video Curriculum
Youth Ministry Outside the Lines: The Dangerous Wonder of Working with Teenagers

STUDENT RESOURCES

Downloading the Bible: A Rough Guide to the New Testament
Downloading the Bible: A Rough Guide to the Old Testament
Grow For It Journal through the Scriptures
So What Am I Gonna Do With My Life? Journaling Workbook for Students
Spiritual Challenge Journal: The Next Level
Teen Devotional Bible
What (Almost) Nobody Will Tell You about Sex
What Would Jesus Do? Spiritual Challenge Journal
Wild Truth Journal for Junior Highers
Wild Truth Journal—Pictures of God
Wild Truth Journal—Pictures of God 2

SO YOU WANNA GET YOUR KIDS TALKING ABOUT REAL-LIFE ISSUES?

Then don't miss the full set of updated TalkSheets!

JUNIOR HIGH • MIDDLE SCHOOL
TALKSHEETS—UPDATED!

MORE JUNIOR HIGH • MIDDLE
SCHOOL TALKSHEETS—UPDATED!

JUNIOR HIGH • MIDDLE
SCHOOL TALKSHEETS PSALMS &
PROVERBS—UPDATED!

HIGH SCHOOL TALKSHEETS—
UPDATED!

MORE HIGH SCHOOL TALKSHEETS—
UPDATED!

HIGH SCHOOL TALKSHEETS
PSALMS & PROVERBS—UPDATED!

www.YouthSpecialties.com